Arrive Math Games Kit

Resource Guide

Mc Graw Hill Education

mheducation.com/prek-12

Copyright © 2019 McGraw-Hill Education

All rights reserved. The contents, or parts thereof, may be reproduced in print form for non-profit educational use with *Arrive Math Games Kit*, provided such reproductions bear copyright notice, but may not be reproduced in any form for any other purpose without the prior written consent of McGraw-Hill Education, including, but not limited to, network storage or transmission, or broadcast for distance learning.

Send all inquiries to:
McGraw-Hill Education
8787 Orion Place
Columbus, OH 43240

ISBN: 978-0-07-684885-0
MHID: 0-07-684885-X

Printed in the United States of America.

4 5 6 7 8 9 10 LHN 24 23 22

Table of Contents

Introduction to *Arrive Math Games Kit* .... vii – ix

Using the Game Instruction Cards x

Teacher Tips xi

List of Games .... xii – xiv

Game Blackline Masters

20 Buckets
20 Buckets Equation Cards 1
20 Buckets Tens Frame 4

How Many Now?
How Many Problems 6

Shape Builder
Shape Builder Outlines 12

Shape Collector
Collector Mat 15

Pony Express
Address Cards 16
Pony Express Number Line 19

Race to the Rescue
Race to the Rescue Cards 24

Going Shopping
Going Shopping General Store 32
Going Shopping Record Sheet 34

Mystery Measuring
Measuring Record Sheet 35

Fill It Up
Shape Outlines 36

Drop the Counter
Drop the Counter Bar Graph 39

500 Here I Come!
Here I Come! Construction Mat 40

100 Buckets to Victory
Equation Record Sheet 41

Games Kit Resource Guide • Table of Contents iii

Gopher It!
Gopher It! Record Sheet.. 42

Measurement Hunt
Measurement Hunt Record Sheet... 43

Shape Bingo
Blank Bingo Mat 44
Shape Bingo Cards... 45
Shape Bingo Mat 46

Fruit Collector
Fruit Cards.. 50
Fruit Collector Bar Graph 51
Fruit Collector Picture Graph 52
Fruit Collector Question Cards.. 53

Riddles in the Labyrinth
Multiplication Table... 54
Riddle Cards... 55

Master Builder
Master Builder Cards 57

Four Sides of Victory
Attribute Cards 59
Quadrilateral Guides 60
Side Lengths... 61

A Scaly Situation
A Scaly Situation Bar Graph.. 62
A Scaly Situation Record Sheet 63
Word Problem Cards... 64

Fraction Frenzy
Fraction Adding Cards.. 66
Fraction Subtracting Cards.. 70

Multiplication Jumble
Jumble Cards 74

Goo-d Alien Research
Customary Research 78
Metric Research 79
Research Cards 80

Attribute Bingo
Attribute Bingo Cards 82
Blank Shape Mat... 83
Shape Mat 84

Collector Challenge
Collection Cards 88
Collection Line Plot... 92

Expanding Trek
Decimal Number Cards 93
Decimal Number Writing Frame 96

Win Sum Lose Sum
Fraction Mat 97
Win Sum Lose Sum Record Sheet 98

The Great Expression Trek
Basic Expression Record Sheet 99
Expression Record Sheet 100

Volume Builder
Volume Mat 101
Volume Record Sheet 102

Got the Plot?
Fraction Sums and Differences 103
Solution Record Sheet 105

Climbing Capture
Climbing Capture Problem Cards 106

Ratio Bingo
Ratio Bingo Cards 110
Ratio Bingo Mat 115

Area Trek
Area Trek Cards 119

Creatures under the Surface
Surface Area Cards 123

Absolutely Rational
Absolutely Rational Record Sheet 130
Rational Number Cards 131

Expression Expert
Expression Expert Cards 137

Ratio Fishing
Ratio Fishing Cards 141
Ratio Fishing Record Sheet 149

Scaling the Job Site
Architectural Blueprints 150
Job Site Cards 152

Circle Circuits
Circle Circuits Record Sheet 156

Star Populations
Population Cards 157

Number Line Fill Up
Number Line Fill Up Cards 166

Counter Capture
Linear Equation Cards 170

Functional Star Chase
Function Cards 178

Turn Up the Volume
Turn Up the Volume Sheet 184

I've Been Transformed!
Transformation Cards with Triangles 185

Scattering Plots
Coordinate Cards..187
Scatter Plot Graph..190
Vote Cards 191

Introduction

Welcome to the *Arrive Math Games Kit!* The games in this kit are designed to engage and help students practice math skills and concepts that they are learning in their math class. Each game is designed for 2–6 players, and the kit includes game boards and hands-on manipulatives for easy game play. Use the Games Kit box to easily organize your games and materials.

What is in the Games Kit?

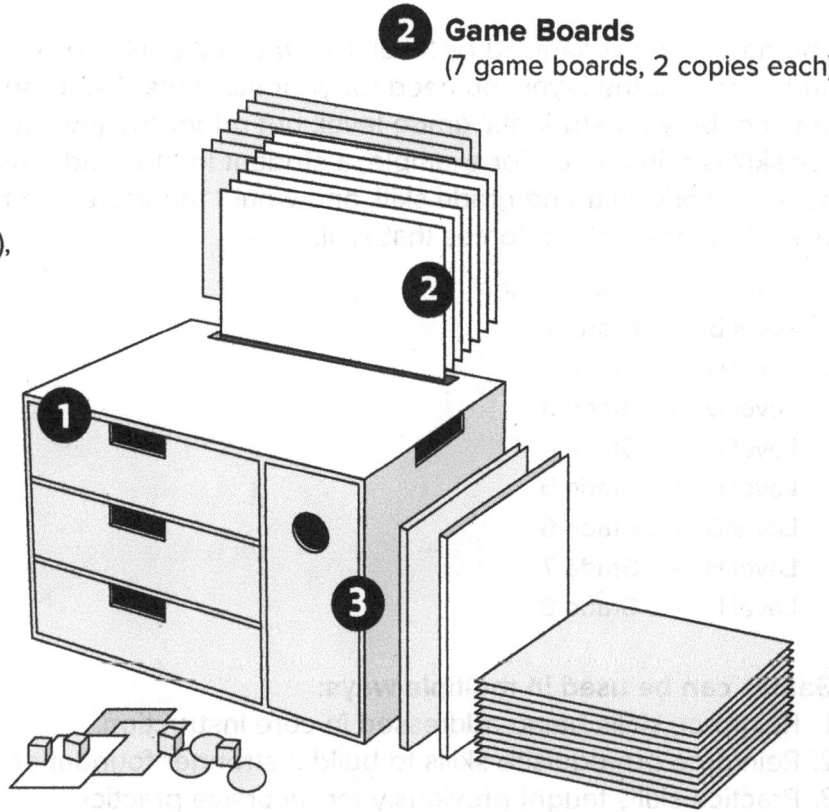

① Manipulatives

Top Drawer:
Fraction tiles (8 sets),
Number cards (6 sets),
Number cube 1–6 (1 set),
Number cube 7–12 (1 set),
Pattern blocks (1 set),
Pawns (2 sets),
Spinner 1–4 (2),
Transparent spinner (2)

Middle Drawer:
Color tiles (4 sets),
Counters (6 sets),
Connecting cubes (1 set)

Bottom Drawer:
Base-ten blocks:
hundred flats (3 sets),
Base-ten blocks:
ten rods (3 sets),
Base-ten blocks:
one units (3 sets)

② Game Boards
(7 game boards, 2 copies each)

③ Resource Guide

The Resource Guide provides an overview to get you started with the *Arrive Math Games Kit.* It includes:
- Implementation suggestions
- List of Games
- Math Focus
- All supporting Blackline Masters for game play

Instruction Cards
(2 sets of 54)

Each Instruction Card provides:
- Directions for game play
- Materials list
- Teacher tips
- Game variations

Game Cards
(2 sets of 2)

The game cards correspond to the Creature Cavern and Urban Trek game boards to support game play.

How can the Games Kit support my students?

Games are used to reinforce math concepts in an engaging way. Students will have the opportunity to practice math skills with their peers while utilizing kinesthetic learning styles and problem-solving skills. Allowing students multiple opportunities to practice math skills in a variety of ways allows them to make deeper connections and strengthen their understanding of math concepts.

How do I know which game to use?

The games are organized by level. Use the List of Games chart to find games at the level you need for your students. The grade level may not be your students' grade level, but rather the level at which the skill is reinforced. For example, a student in 4th grade might need to work on a 2nd grade skill, and would therefore use the Level C game that reinforces that skill.

Level A = Kindergarten
Level B = Grade 1
Level C = Grade 2
Level D = Grade 3
Level E = Grade 4
Level F = Grade 5
Level G = Grade 6
Level H = Grade 7
Level I = Grade 8

Games can be used in multiple ways:
1. Reinforce skills being addressed in core instruction.
2. Reinforce prerequisite skills to build a stronger foundation.
3. Practice skills taught previously for recursive practice.

Class data from students' core math instruction or from use of the *Arrive Math Booster* can also inform game selection.

List of Games
The chart below identifies the math focus reinforced in each game. Use this chart to identify games in each grade level and strand that focus on the math concept you want students to strengthen.

Level	Strand	Math Focus	Game Title
A	Number and Quantity	Count on to 100.	Tunnel to 100
A	Operations	Practice fluency with addition facts to five and count on to 20.	20 Buckets
A	Algebraic Thinking	Solve addition problems within 10 with objects.	How Many Now?
A	Measurement	Describe and compare the measurable attribute of height.	Tallest Tower

Level → (points to Level column)
Strand → (points to Strand column)
Game Title → (points to Game Title column)

viii Games Kit Resource Guide • Introduction

How do I incorporate the Games Kit into my classroom?

There are multiple ways that you can use the Games Kit in your classroom. Here are two recommendations:

1. **Workstations:** If you want all students to practice the same skill, consider using a game during center time when students rotate to different centers in a block of time. Set up a center or workstation with one game. Use a variation of the game in a second center. Explain the game before students begin the rotation. Provide all materials that are needed for the game. Students can work in groups of 2–6 depending on the game.

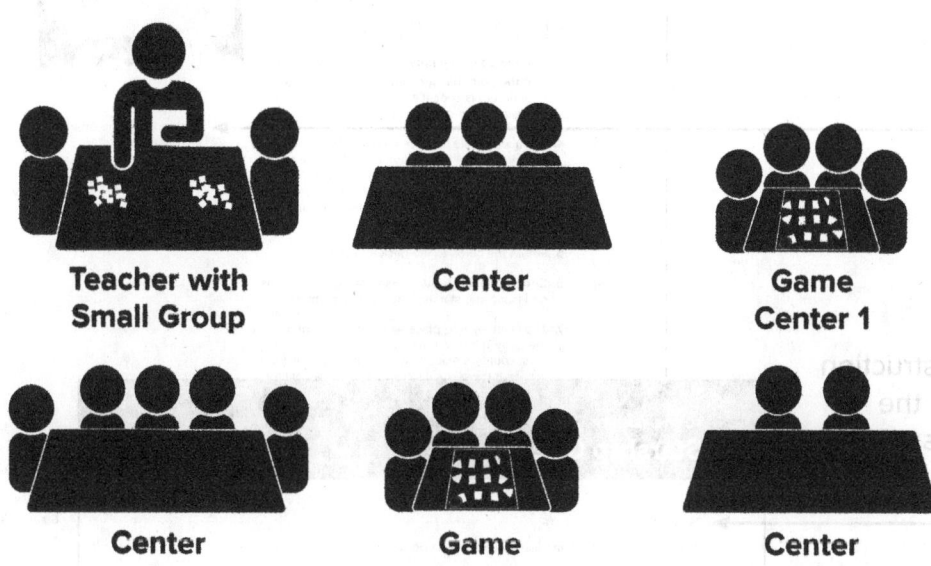

2. **Class Game Time:** Set up small groups for the entire class to participate in game play at one time. Each group can practice different skills by using different games. There are two copies of each game board, so you can have two groups working on the same game at one time.

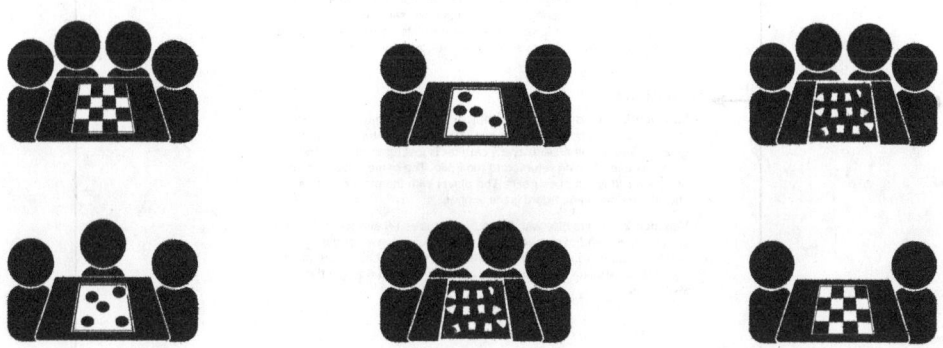

Using the Game Instruction Cards

Each two-sided Instruction Card has support for both students and teachers.

The front of each Instruction Card is designed for students and includes:

Game Objective

Game Play Directions

Materials List

The back of each Instruction Card is designed for the teacher and includes:

Math Focus

Instructions for Set-Up

Tips for Game Play

Variations for Game Play

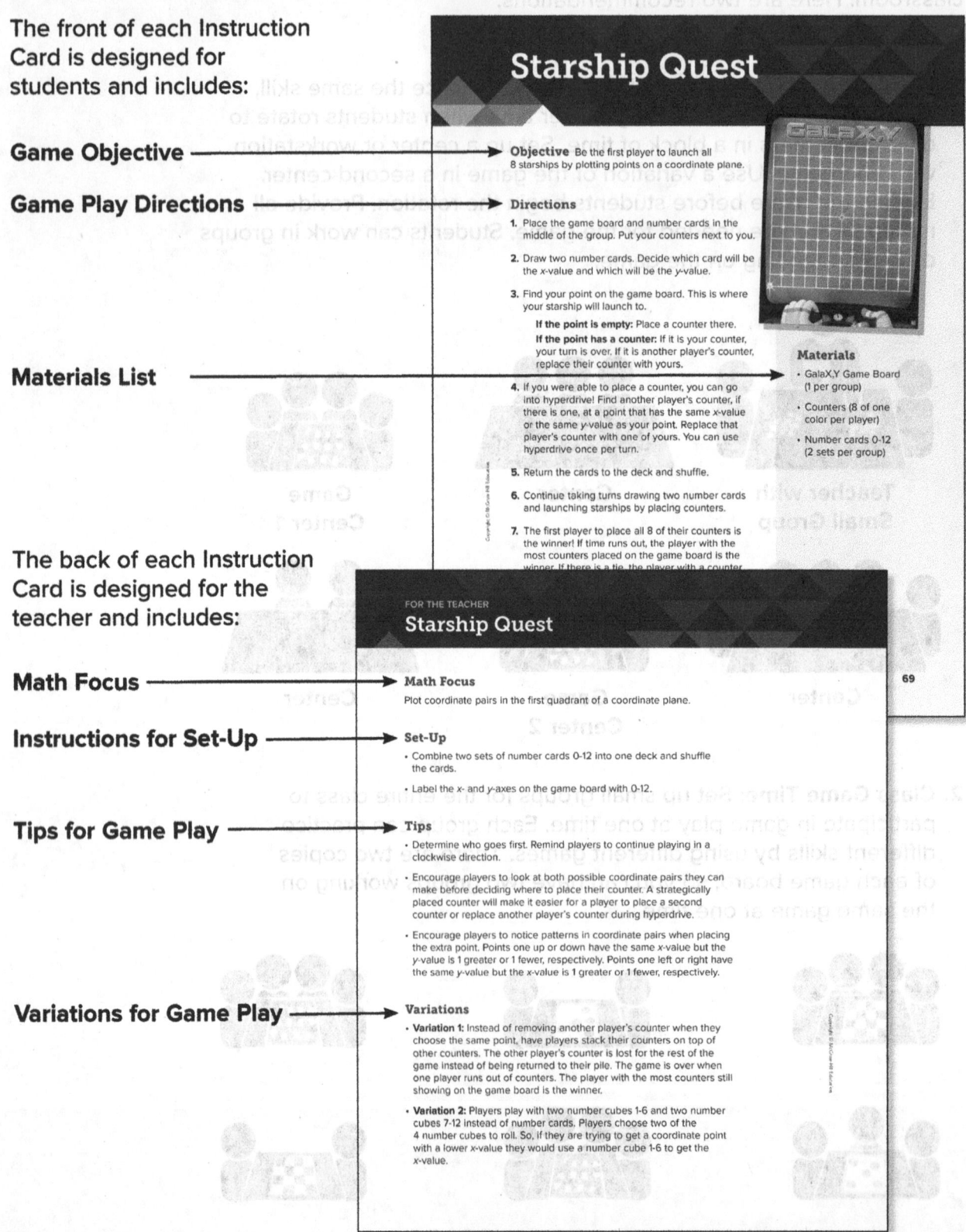

Starship Quest

Objective Be the first player to launch all 8 starships by plotting points on a coordinate plane.

Directions

1. Place the game board and number cards in the middle of the group. Put your counters next to you.
2. Draw two number cards. Decide which card will be the *x*-value and which will be the *y*-value.
3. Find your point on the game board. This is where your starship will launch to.
   If the point is empty: Place a counter there.
   If the point has a counter: If it is your counter, your turn is over. If it is another player's counter, replace their counter with yours.
4. If you were able to place a counter, you can go into hyperdrive! Find another player's counter, if there is one, at a point that has the same *x*-value or the same *y*-value as your point. Replace that player's counter with one of yours. You can use hyperdrive once per turn.
5. Return the cards to the deck and shuffle.
6. Continue taking turns drawing two number cards and launching starships by placing counters.
7. The first player to place all 8 of their counters is the winner! If time runs out, the player with the most counters placed on the game board is the winner. If there is a tie, the player with a counter

Materials
- GalaX,Y Game Board (1 per group)
- Counters (8 of one color per player)
- Number cards 0-12 (2 sets per group)

FOR THE TEACHER
Starship Quest

Math Focus
Plot coordinate pairs in the first quadrant of a coordinate plane.

Set-Up
- Combine two sets of number cards 0-12 into one deck and shuffle the cards.
- Label the *x*- and *y*-axes on the game board with 0-12.

Tips
- Determine who goes first. Remind players to continue playing in a clockwise direction.
- Encourage players to look at both possible coordinate pairs they can make before deciding where to place their counter. A strategically placed counter will make it easier for a player to place a second counter or replace another player's counter during hyperdrive.
- Encourage players to notice patterns in coordinate pairs when placing the extra point. Points one up or down have the same *x*-value but the *y*-value is 1 greater or 1 fewer, respectively. Points one left or right have the same *y*-value but the *x*-value is 1 greater or 1 fewer, respectively.

Variations
- **Variation 1:** Instead of removing another player's counter when they choose the same point, have players stack their counters on top of other counters. The other player's counter is lost for the rest of the game instead of being returned to their pile. The game is over when one player runs out of counters. The player with the most counters still showing on the game board is the winner.
- **Variation 2:** Players play with two number cubes 1-6 and two number cubes 7-12 instead of number cards. Players choose two of the 4 number cubes to roll. So, if they are trying to get a coordinate point with a lower *x*-value they would use a number cube 1-6 to get the *x*-value.

Teacher Tips

The games are designed to engage students and reinforce math skills. Students may have varying levels of experience playing games in the classroom. These teacher tips will help game play run more smoothly.

1. **Prepare games ahead of time.**
   - Prepare materials early in the year so that the games are ready when you need them.
   - Read and familiarize yourself with the games before your students play so that you can provide guidance or adapt instructions to your students' needs.
   - Play games in advance with a small group to help you understand areas where students may need extra support.

2. **Guide students on how to determine who goes first, such as:**
   - Roll a number cube. The greatest number goes first.
   - Pick a card from the number card deck. The greatest number goes first.
   - Continue taking turns clockwise.

3. **Hold students accountable for demonstrating learning.**
   - Have students record their calculations on paper.
   - Have students write a reflection about the game.
   - Have students check each other's work when appropriate.

4. **Model game play.**
   - When introducing a new game, model the game with a small group of students while the rest of the group observes.
   - Write examples on the board to offer further support.

List of Games

The chart below identifies the math focus reinforced in each game. Use this chart to identify games in each grade level and strand that focus on the math concept you want students to strengthen.

Level	Strand	Math Focus	Game Title
A	Number and Quantity	Count on to 100.	Tunnel to 100
A	Operations	Practice fluency with addition facts to five and count on to 20.	20 Buckets
A	Algebraic Thinking	Solve addition problems within 10 with objects.	How Many Now?
A	Measurement	Describe and compare the measurable attribute of height.	Tallest Tower
A	Geometry	Create composite shapes.	Shape Builder
A	Statistical Analysis	Classify objects and count the number within each category.	Shape Collector
B	Number and Quantity	Understand place value to 100 by skip counting by tens and ones.	Pony Express
B	Operations	Add and subtract to 10.	Race to the Rescue
B	Algebraic Thinking	Represent and solve problems involving addition.	Going Shopping
B	Measurement	Measure length using nonstandard objects.	Mystery Measuring
B	Geometry	Identify shape attributes and create composite shapes.	Fill It Up
B	Statistical Analysis	Record and interpret data in a bar graph.	Drop the Counter
C	Number and Quantity	Regroup to understand place value to three digits.	500 Here I Come!
C	Operations	Add and subtract to solve problems to 100.	100 Buckets to Victory
C	Algebraic Thinking	Solve word problems involving addition and subtraction to 100.	Gopher It!
C	Measurement	Estimate the length of paper strips, and then measure them in inches.	Measurement Hunt
C	Geometry	Recognize shapes by their attributes.	Shape Bingo
C	Statistical Analysis	Create and interpret bar and picture graphs that represent data sets.	Fruit Collector

Level	Strand	Math Focus	Game Title
D	Number and Quantity	Build fractions equivalent to one.	Trek to 1
D	Operations	Multiply within 36.	Space Pioneer
D	Algebraic Thinking	Identify and explain arithmetic patterns in multiplication up to 10 × 10.	Riddles in the Labyrinth
D	Measurement	Use multiplication to find the areas of rectangles and non-overlapping composite shapes.	Master Builder
D	Geometry	Use attributes to build quadrilaterals, such as parallelograms, squares, rectangles, rhombuses, and trapezoids.	Four Sides of Victory
D	Statistical Analysis	Construct and interpret scaled bar graphs representing word problems.	A Scaly Situation
E	Number and Quantity	Compare two multi-digit numbers.	A-Mazing Place Value
E	Operations	Find the sum of two fractions.	Fraction Frenzy
E	Algebraic Thinking	Use factors and products to create multiplication equations.	Multiplication Jumble
E	Measurement	Convert larger measurement units into smaller measurement units.	Goo-d Alien Research
E	Geometry	Identify attributes of shapes.	Attribute Bingo
E	Statistical Analysis	Plot measurements to eighths and interpret the differences between measurements using a line plot.	Collector Challenge
F	Number and Quantity	Write decimal numbers in expanded form.	Expanding Trek
F	Operations	Find the sum of two fractions.	Win Sum Lose Sum
F	Algebraic Thinking	Write and evaluate algebraic expressions.	The Great Expression Trek
F	Measurement	Use the volume formula to calculate the volume of rectangular prisms.	Volume Builder
F	Geometry	Plot coordinate pairs in the first quadrant of a coordinate plane.	Starship Quest
F	Statistical Analysis	Make line plots to display data to eighths.	Got the Plot?
G	Number and Quantity	Find the greatest common factor of two whole numbers.	Greatest Common Foe

Level	Strand	Math Focus	Game Title
G	Operations	Understand positive and negative numbers and plot them on a number line.	Climbing Capture
G	Algebraic Thinking	Understand the concept of ratio and unit rate.	Ratio Bingo
G	Measurement	Find the areas of shapes.	Area Trek
G	Geometry	Find the surface area of three-dimensional figures.	Creatures under the Surface
G	Statistical Analysis	Understand and calculate measures of center.	Don't Be Mean, Data!
H	Number and Quantity	Apply and extend understanding of rational numbers.	Absolutely Rational
H	Operations	Evaluate expressions using properties of operations.	Expression Expert
H	Algebraic Thinking	Analyze proportional relationships and calculate unit rates.	Ratio Fishing
H	Measurement	Solve problems involving scale drawings of figures.	Scaling the Job Site
H	Geometry	Find the circumference and area of a circle given the radius.	Circle Circuits
H	Statistical Analysis	Find the median or range to compare two populations.	Star Populations
I	Number and Quantity	Approximate rational and irrational numbers.	Number Line Fill Up
I	Operations	Solve linear equations.	Counter Capture
I	Algebraic Thinking	Compare linear functions.	Functional Star Chase
I	Measurement	Apply the formulas for volumes of cones, cylinders, and spheres.	Turn Up the Volume
I	Geometry	Identify and describe transformations.	I've Been Transformed!
I	Statistical Analysis	Create and interpret scatter plots.	Scattering Plots

20 Buckets Equation Cards

1 + 1	2 + 1	3 + 2	0 + 3
1 + 2	2 + 2	4 + 1	4 + 0
1 + 3	2 + 3	0 + 1	0 + 5
1 + 4	3 + 1	2 + 0	5 + 0
2 + 3			
1 + 4			

20 Buckets Equation Cards

1 + 1	2 + 1	3 + 2	0 + 3
1 + 2	2 + 2	4 + 1	4 + 0
1 + 3	2 + 3	0 + 1	0 + 5
1 + 4	3 + 1	2 + 0	5 + 0
2 + 3			
1 + 4			

20 Buckets Equation Cards

1 + 1	2 + 1	3 + 2	0 + 3
1 + 2	2 + 2	4 + 1	4 + 0
1 + 3	2 + 3	0 + 1	0 + 5
1 + 4	3 + 1	2 + 0	5 + 0
2 + 3			
1 + 4			

20 Buckets Tens Frame

20 Buckets Tens Frame

How Many Problems

There are 5 dogs in the yard.

2 dogs join them.

How many dogs are there in all?

There are 6 dogs in the yard.

1 dog joins them.

How many dogs are there in all?

There are 2 dogs in the yard.

2 dogs join them.

How many dogs are there in all?

There is 1 cat in the yard.

1 cat joins it.

How many cats are there in all?

There are 8 cats in the yard.

2 cats join them.

How many cats are there in all?

There are 3 cats in the yard.

5 cats join them.

How many cats are there in all?

There are 9 birds in the tree.

1 bird joins them.

How many birds are there in all?

There are 2 birds in the tree.

7 birds join them.

How many birds are there in all?

How Many Problems

There is 1 bird in the tree.

3 birds join it.

How many birds are there in all?

There are 6 bugs in the jar.

2 bugs join them.

How many bugs are there in all?

There are 4 bugs in the jar.

5 bugs join them.

How many bugs are there in all?

There is 1 bug in the jar.

6 bugs join it.

How many bugs are there in all?

There are 4 worms in the yard.

4 worms join them.

How many worms are there in all?

There are 2 worms in the yard.

4 worms join them.

How many worms are there in all?

There are 7 worms in the yard.

3 worms join them.

How many worms are there in all?

There are 6 dogs on the rug.

3 dogs join them.

How many dogs are there in all?

How Many Problems

There are 7 dogs on the rug. 1 dog joins them. How many dogs are there in all?	There are 2 dogs on the rug. 3 dogs join them. How many dogs are there in all?
There are 5 cats in the box. 5 cats join them. How many cats are there in all?	There are 3 cats in the box. 2 cats join them. How many cats are there in all?
There are 5 cats in the box. 1 cat joins them. How many cats are there in all?	There is 1 girl in the pool. 8 girls join her. How many girls are there in all?
There are 5 girls in the pool. 3 girls join them. How many girls are there in all?	There are 7 girls in the pool. 2 girls join them. How many girls are there in all?

How Many Problems

There is 1 boy in the pool.

7 boys join him.

How many boys are there in all?

There are 2 boys in the pool.

6 boys join them.

How many boys are there in all?

There are 3 boys in the pool.

4 boys join them.

How many boys are there in all?

There are 4 girls in the room.

3 girls join them.

How many girls are there in all?

There are 3 girls in the room.

3 girls join them.

How many girls are there in all?

There are 3 girls in the room.

7 girls join them.

How many girls are there in all?

There are 2 boys in the room.

1 boy joins them.

How many boys are there in all?

There are 3 boys in the room.

6 boys join them.

How many boys are there in all?

How Many Problems

There is 1 boy in the room.

4 boys join him.

How many boys are there in all?

There is 1 worm in the grass.

2 worms join it.

How many worms are there in all?

There are 3 worms in the grass.

1 worm joins them.

How many worms are there in all?

There are 5 worms in the grass.

4 worms join them.

How many worms are there in all?

There are 2 birds in the yard.

5 birds join them.

How many birds are there in all?

There are 2 birds in the yard.

2 birds join them.

How many birds are there in all?

There are 4 birds in the yard.

1 bird joins them.

How many birds are there in all?

There are 4 lions in the yard.

2 lions join them.

How many lions are there in all?

How Many Problems

There are 8 lions in the yard.

1 lion joins them.

How many lions are there in all?

There is 1 lion in the yard.

9 lions join it.

How many lions are there in all?

There are 6 kittens in the box.

4 kittens join them.

How many kittens are there in all?

There are 4 kittens in the box.

6 kittens join them.

How many kittens are there in all?

There is 1 kitten in the box.

5 kittens join it.

How many kittens are there in all?

There are 2 frogs in the water.

8 frogs join them.

How many frogs are there in all?

There are 7 frogs in the water.

2 frogs join them.

How many frogs are there in all?

There are 6 frogs in the water.

3 frogs join them.

How many frogs are there in all?

Shape Builder Outlines

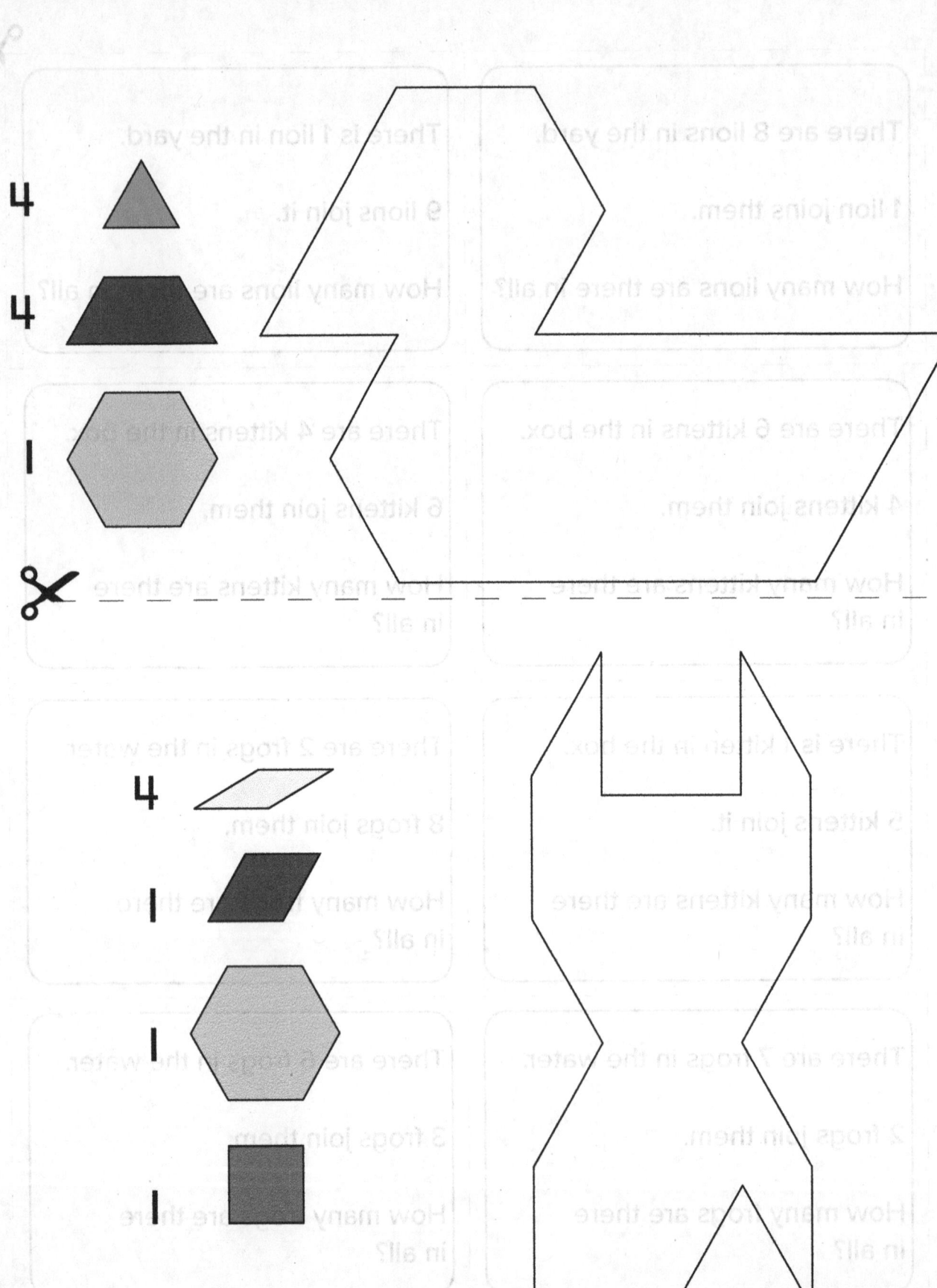

12 Shape Builder Outlines (1 of 3) • Games Kit Resource Guide

Shape Builder Outlines

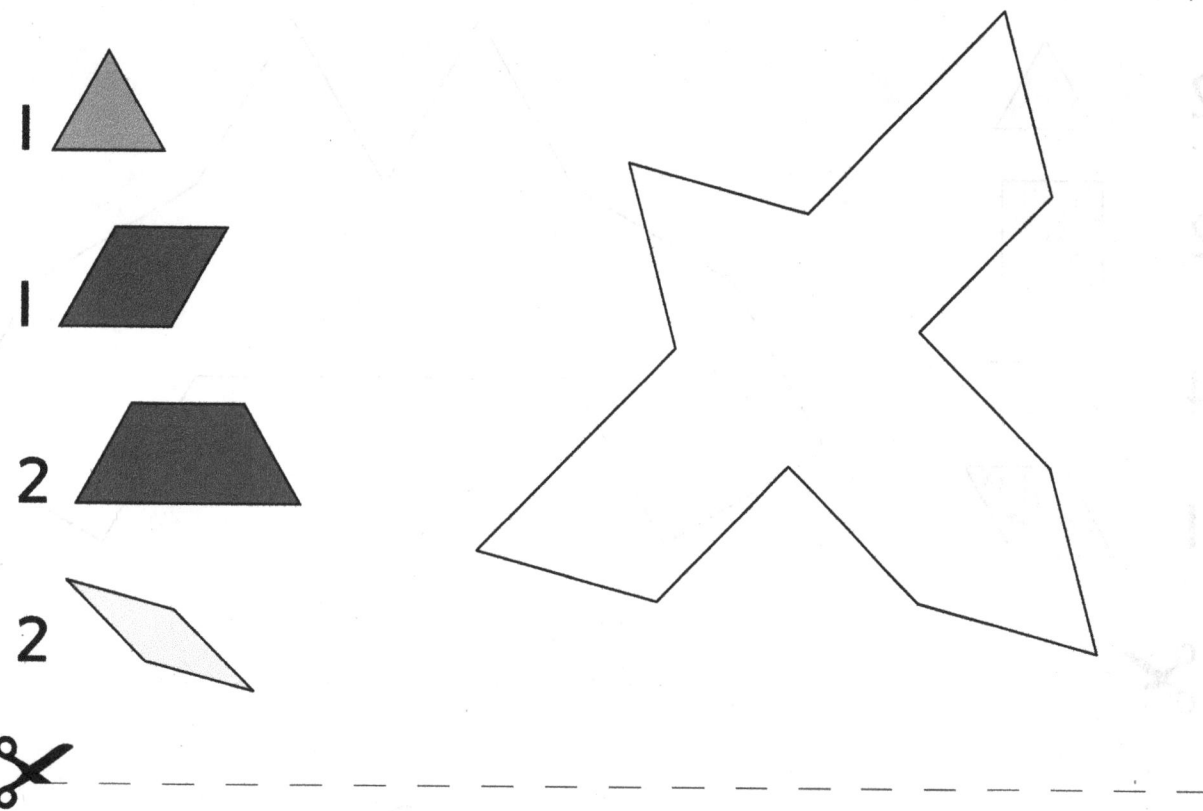

Shape Builder Outlines

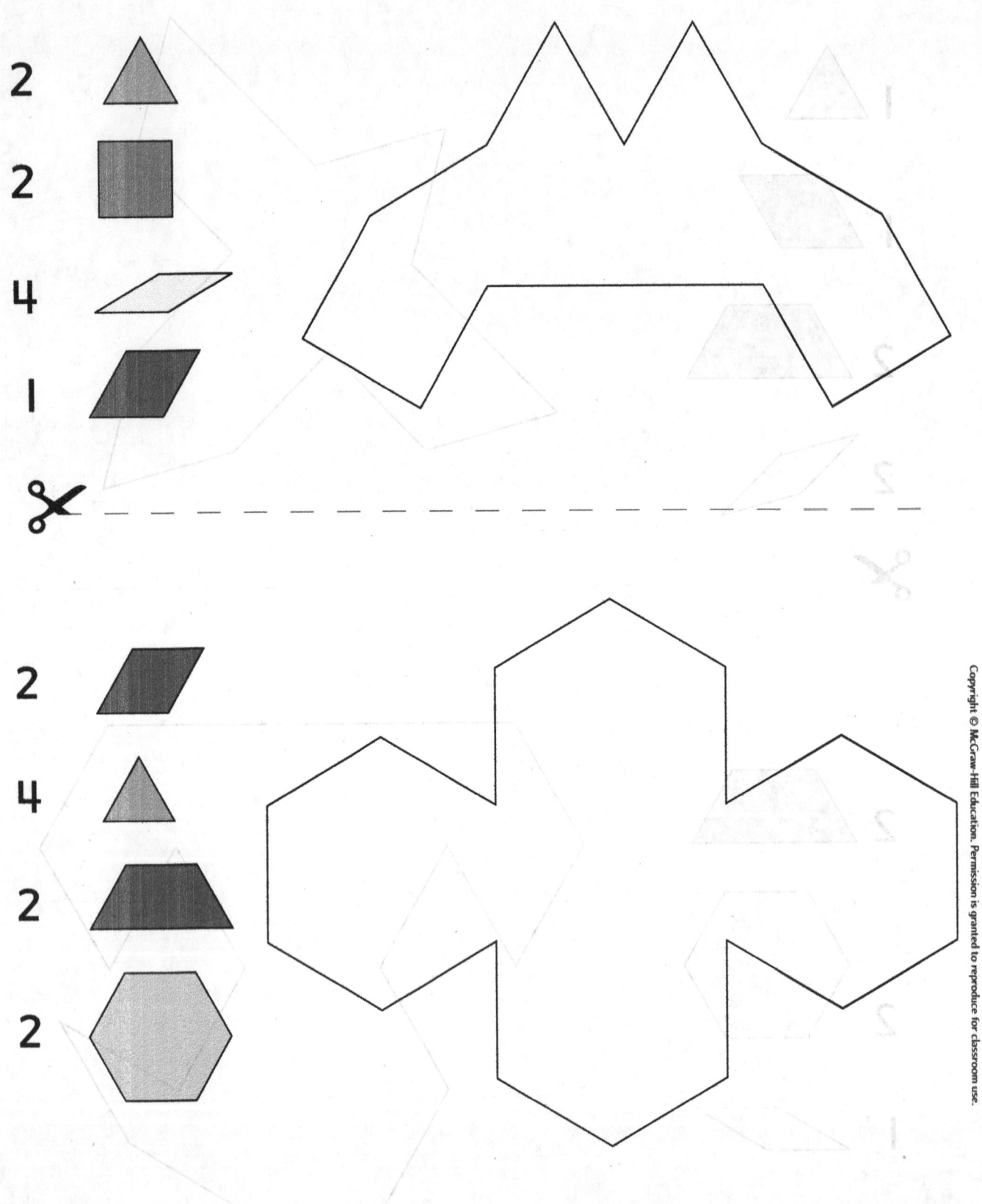

14 Shape Builder Outlines (3 of 3) • Games Kit Resource Guide

Collector Mat

Address Cards

16 Address Cards (1 of 3) • **Games Kit Resource Guide**

Address Cards

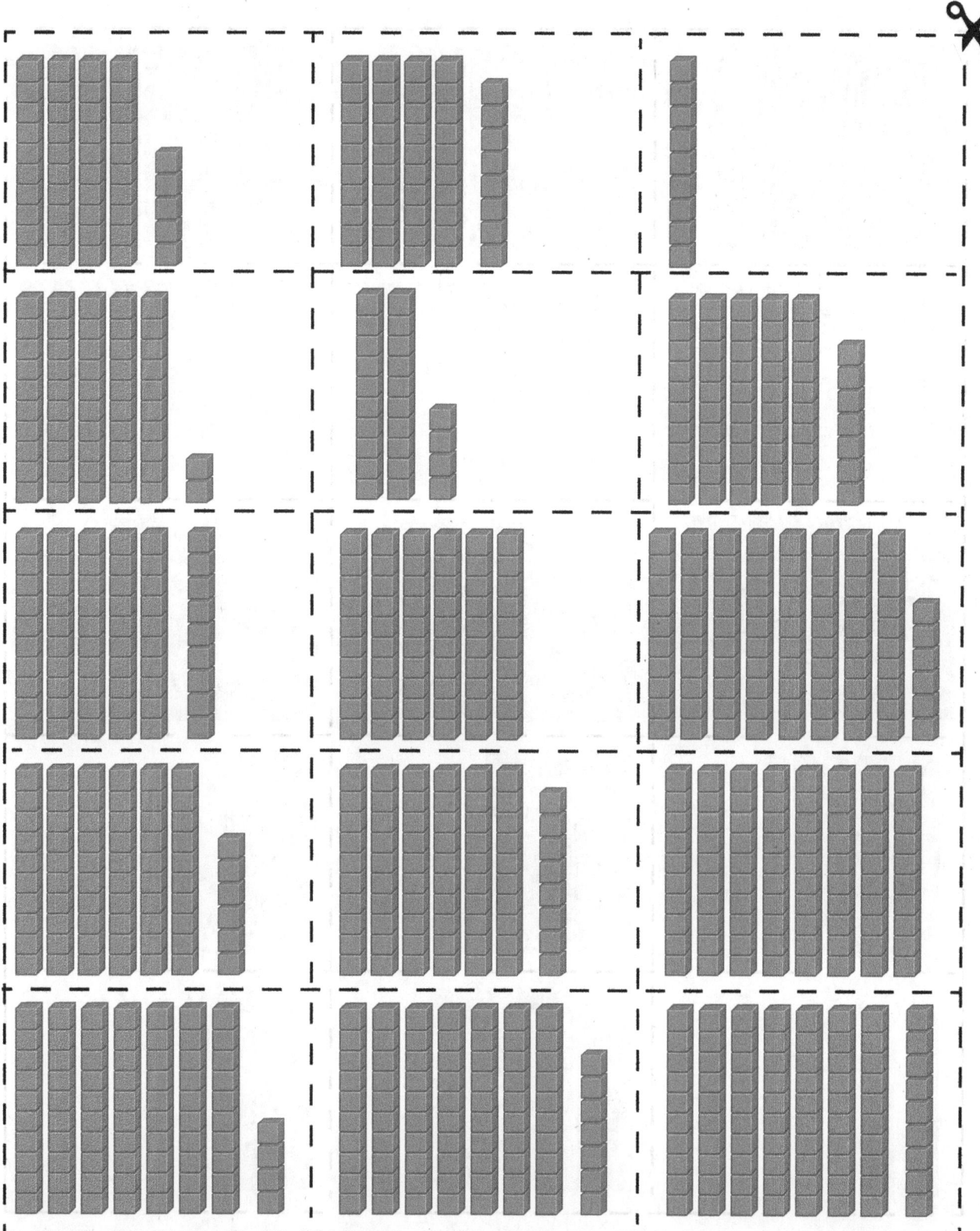

Address Cards

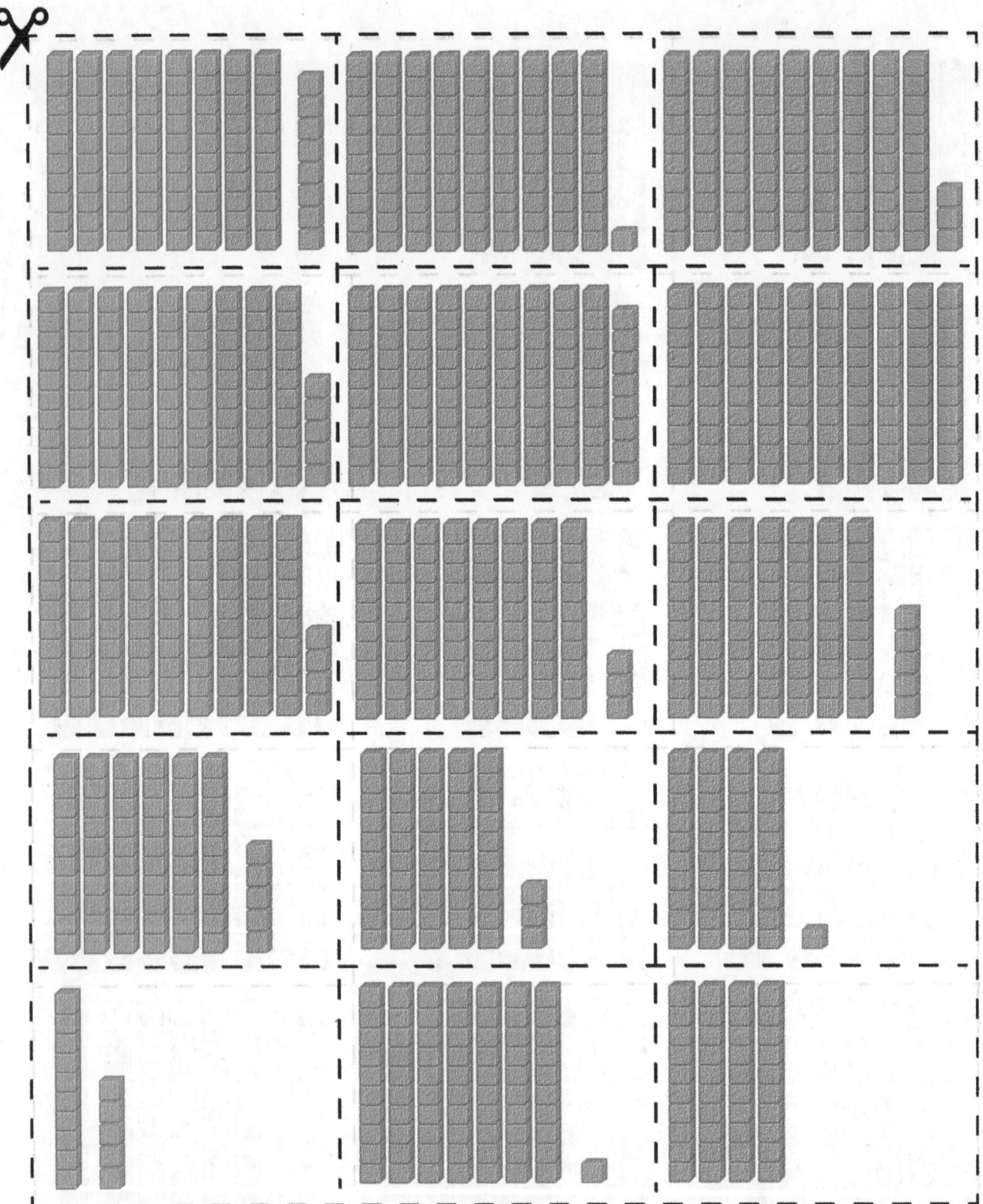

Pony Express Number Line

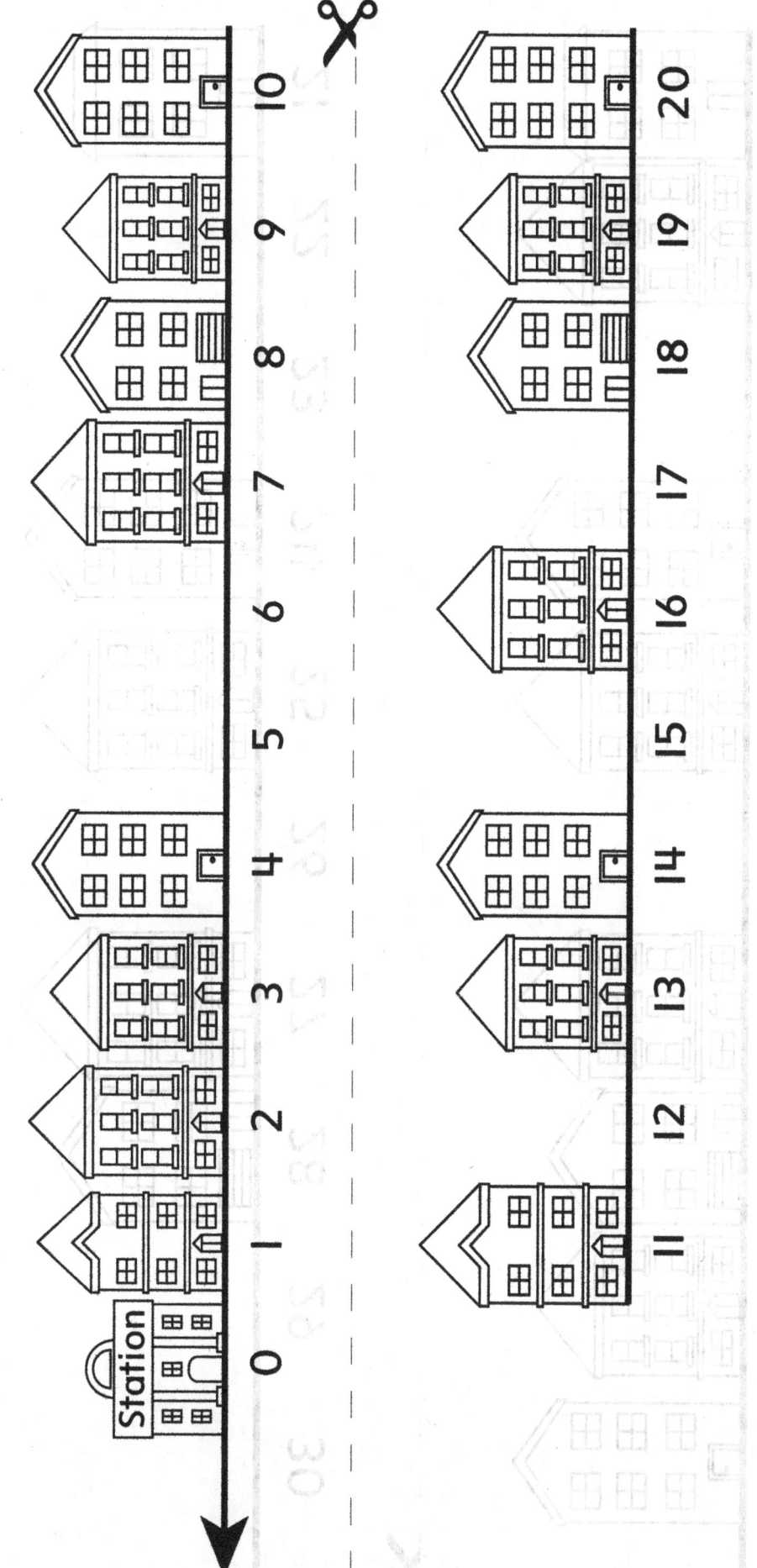

Games Kit Resource Guide • Pony Express Number Line (1 of 5)

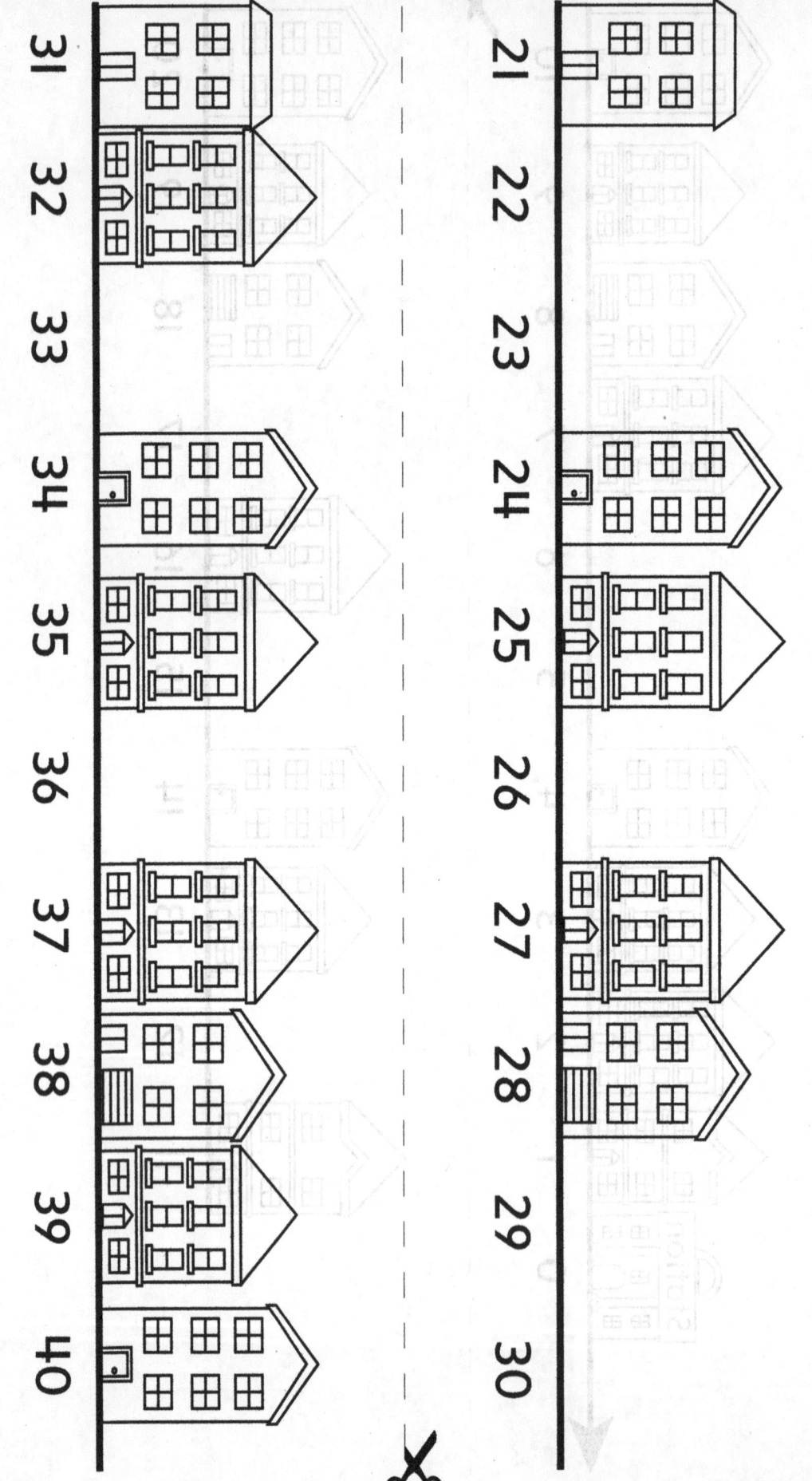

Pony Express Number Line

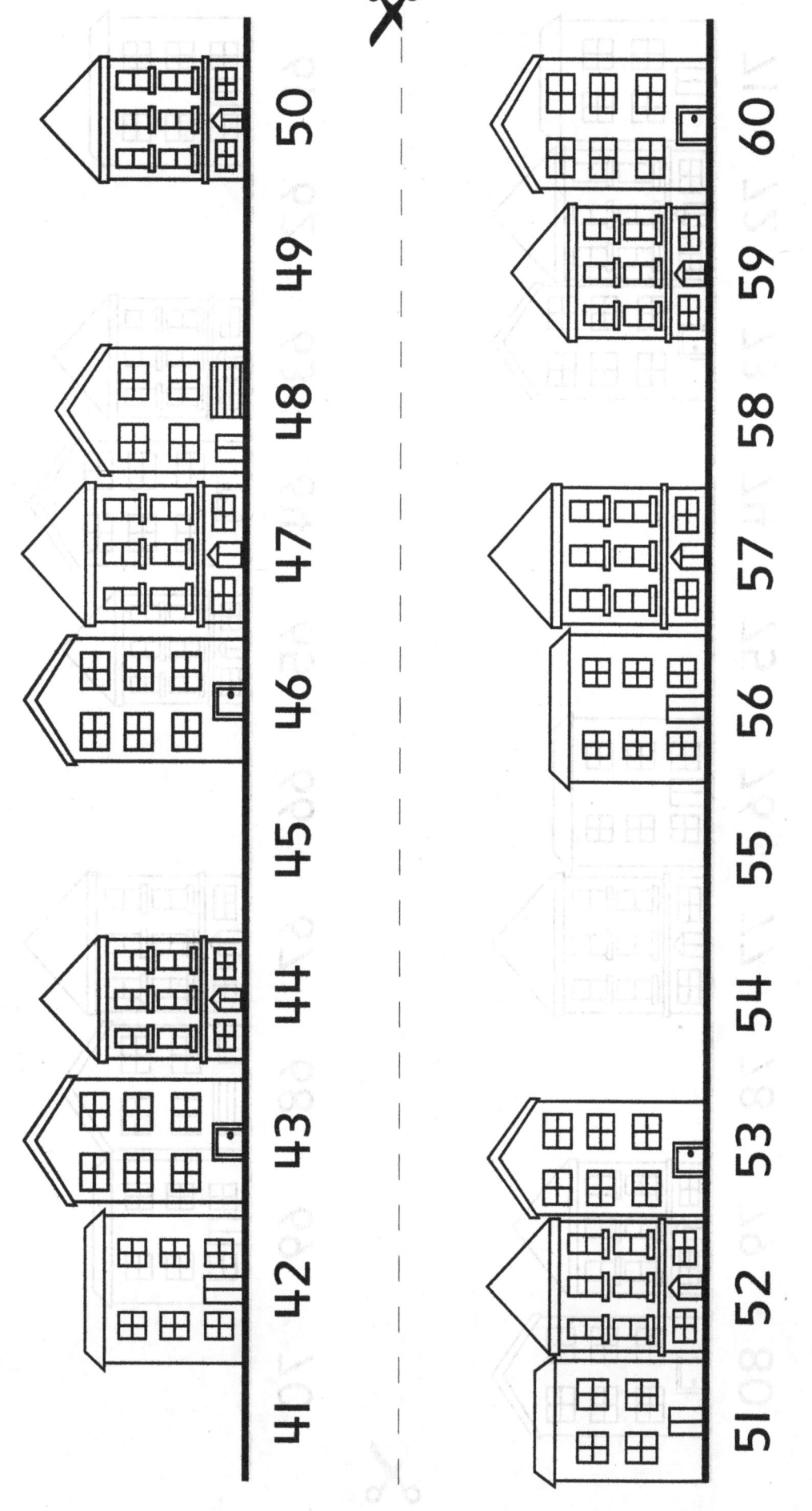

Pony Express Number Line

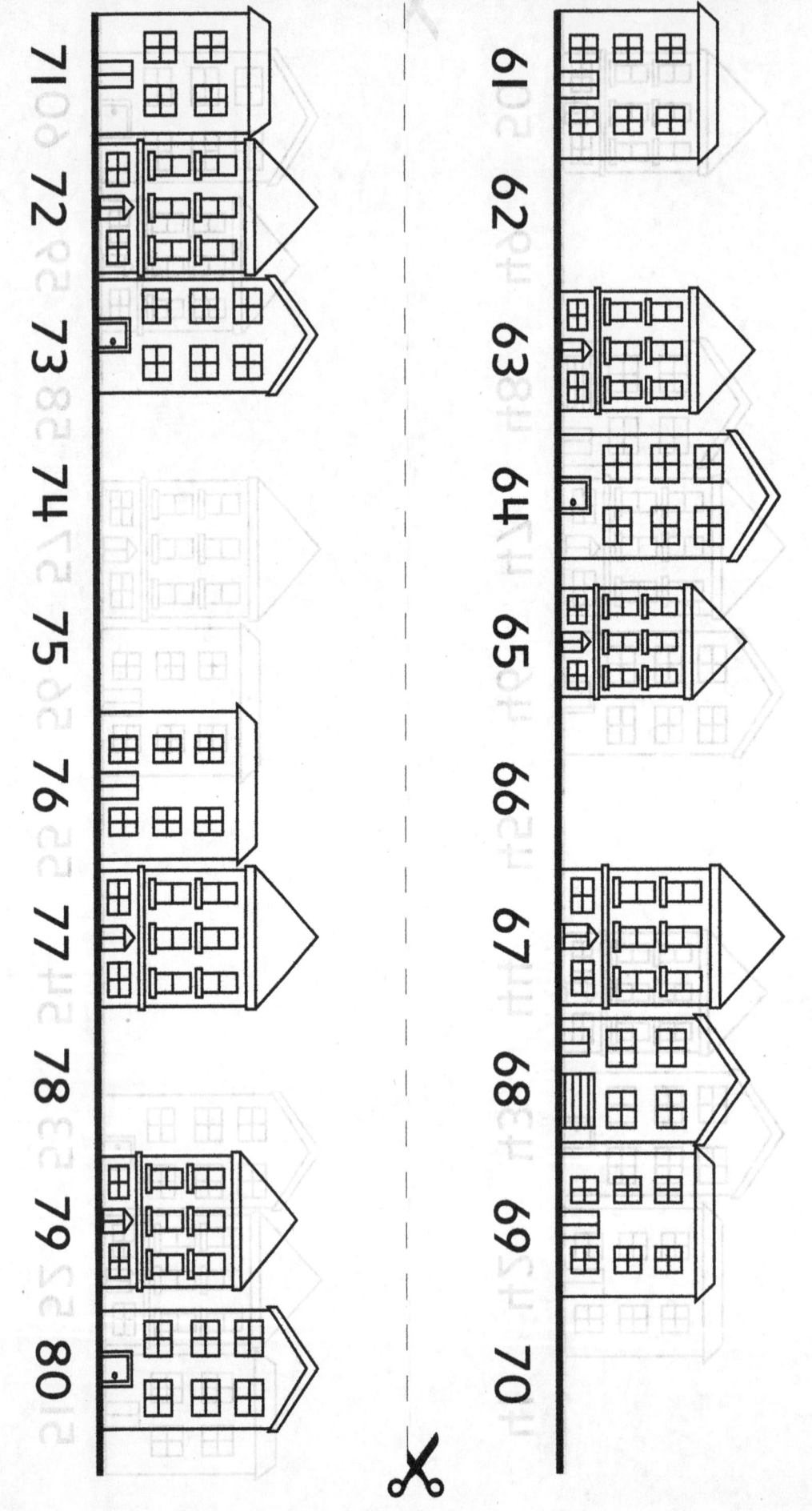

Pony Express Number Line

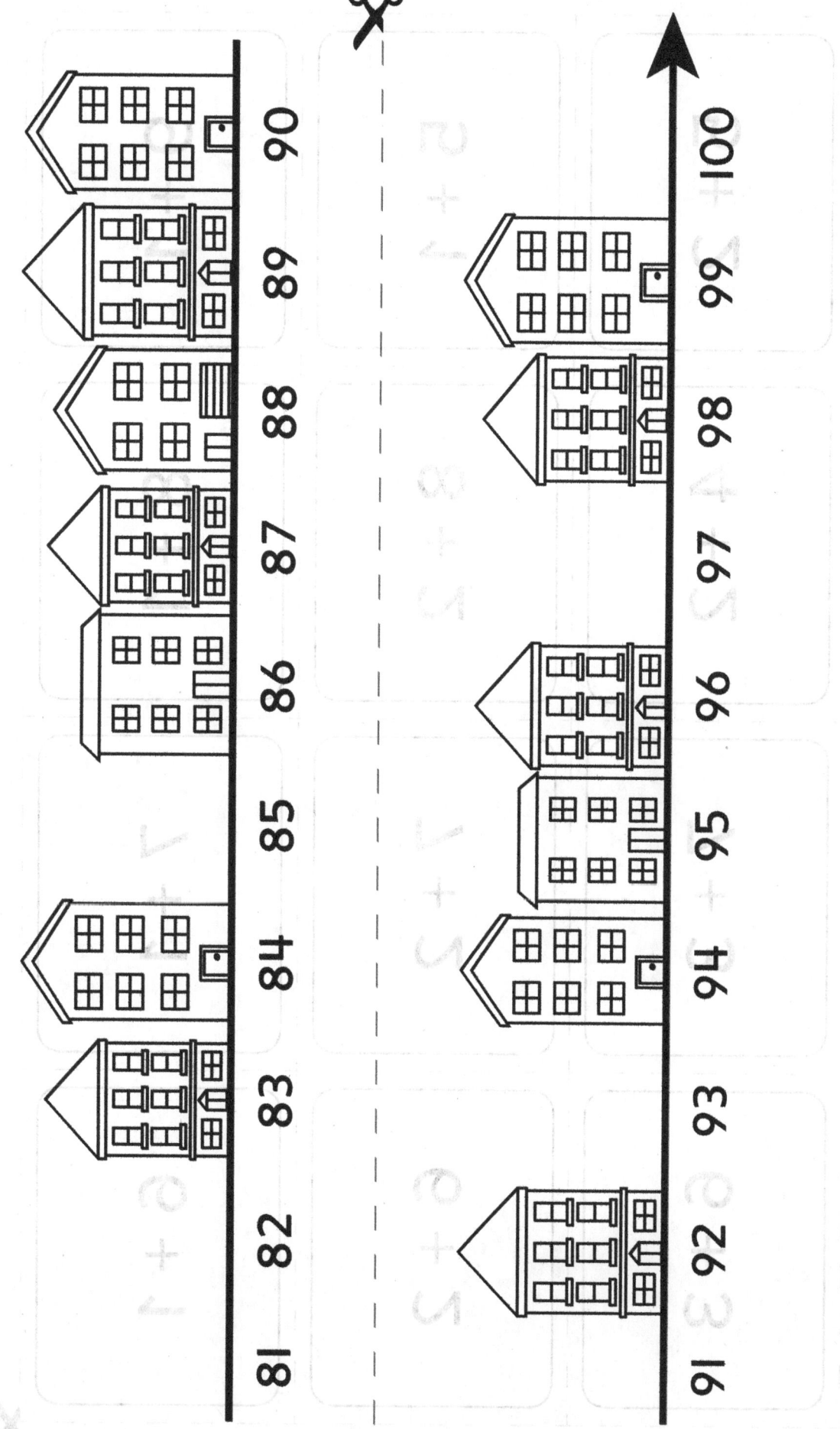

Race to the Rescue Cards

9 + 1	5 + 1	5 + 2
8 + 1	8 + 2	4 + 2
7 + 1	7 + 2	7 + 3
6 + 1	6 + 2	6 + 3

Race to the Rescue Cards

4 + 3	3 + 3	2 + 3	0 + 3
0 + 2	6 + 4	5 + 4	4 + 4
3 + 4	2 + 4	0 + 4	5 + 5

Race to the Rescue Cards

4 + 5	4 + 5	3 + 6
3 + 5	4 + 3	3 + 5
2 + 5	4 + 0	3 + 4
4 + 6	3 + 7	2 + 8

Race to the Rescue Cards

2 + 3	1 + 2	9 – 5
2 + 4	1 + 3	9 – 8
2 + 6	1 + 4	9 – 3
2 + 7	2 + 2	1 + 1

Race to the Rescue Cards

10 − 1	10 − 5	9 − 1
10 − 2	10 − 7	9 − 2
10 − 3	10 − 8	9 − 3
10 − 4	10 − 9	9 − 5

Race to the Rescue Cards

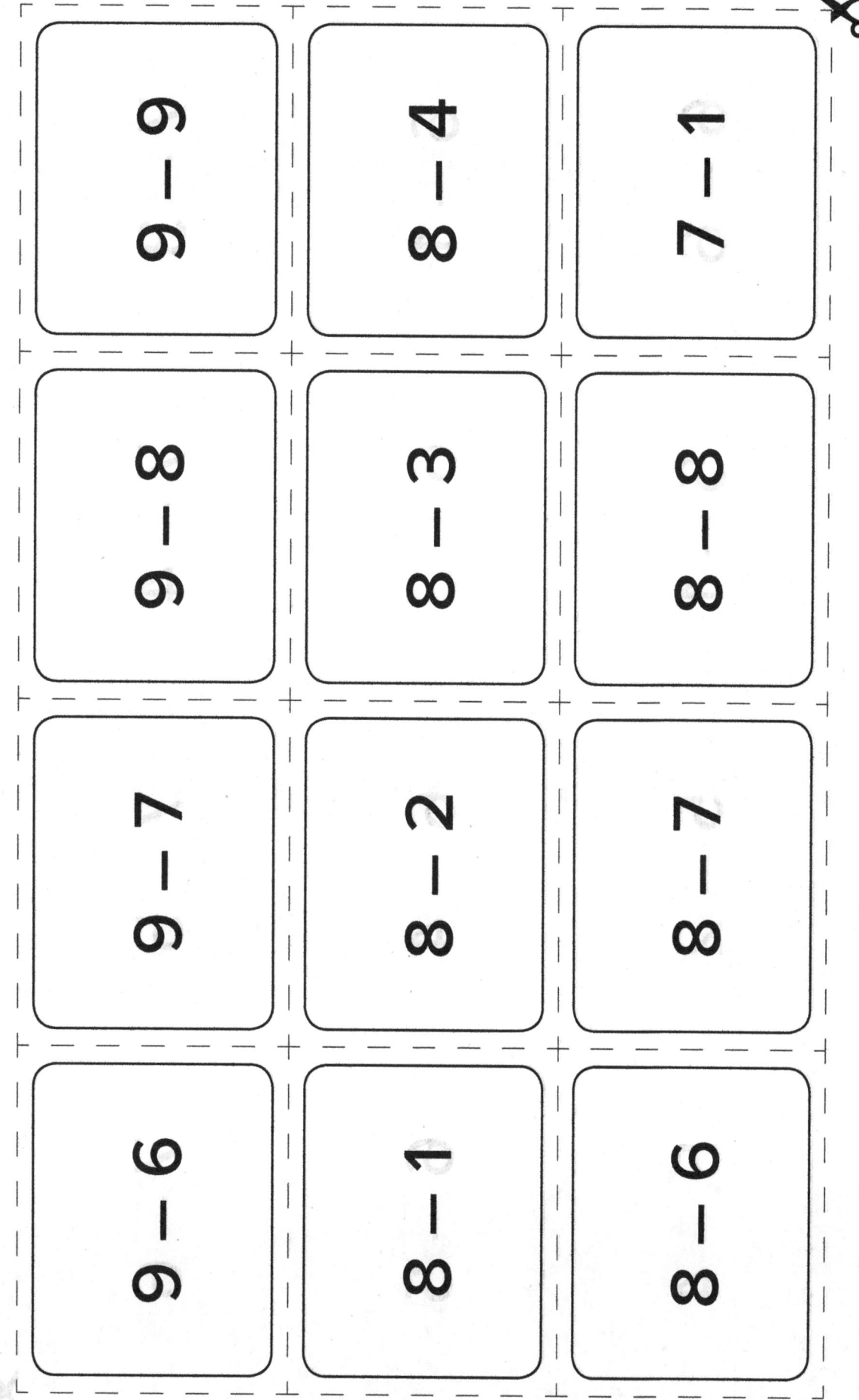

Race to the Rescue Cards

7 − 3	6 − 1	6 − 6
7 − 4	6 − 3	5 − 1
7 − 5	6 − 4	5 − 2
7 − 6	6 − 5	5 − 4

Race to the Rescue Cards

4 − 4	2 − 1	
4 − 2	3 − 3	
4 − 1	3 − 2	
5 − 5	3 − 1	2 − 2

Going Shopping General Store

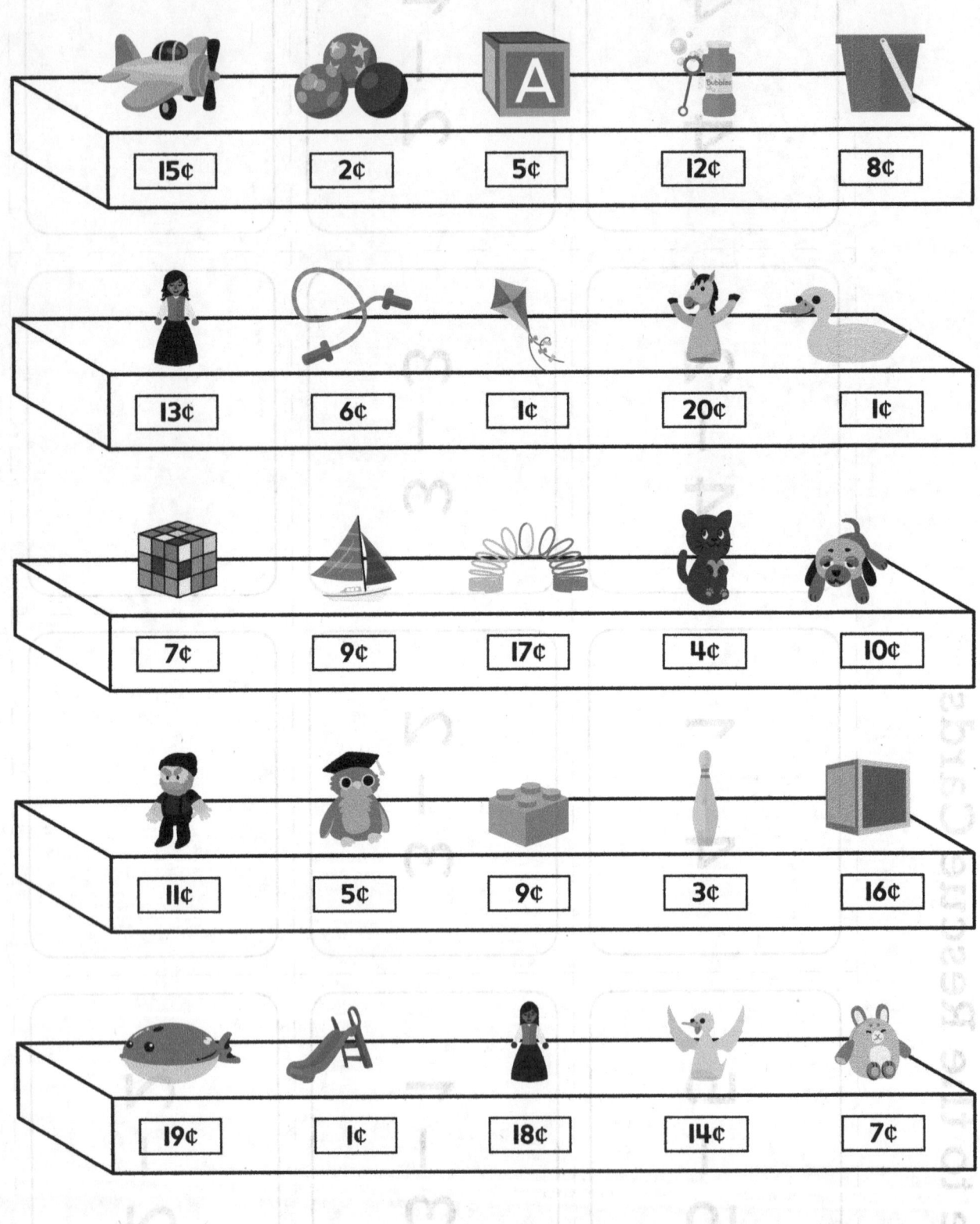

Going Shopping General Store

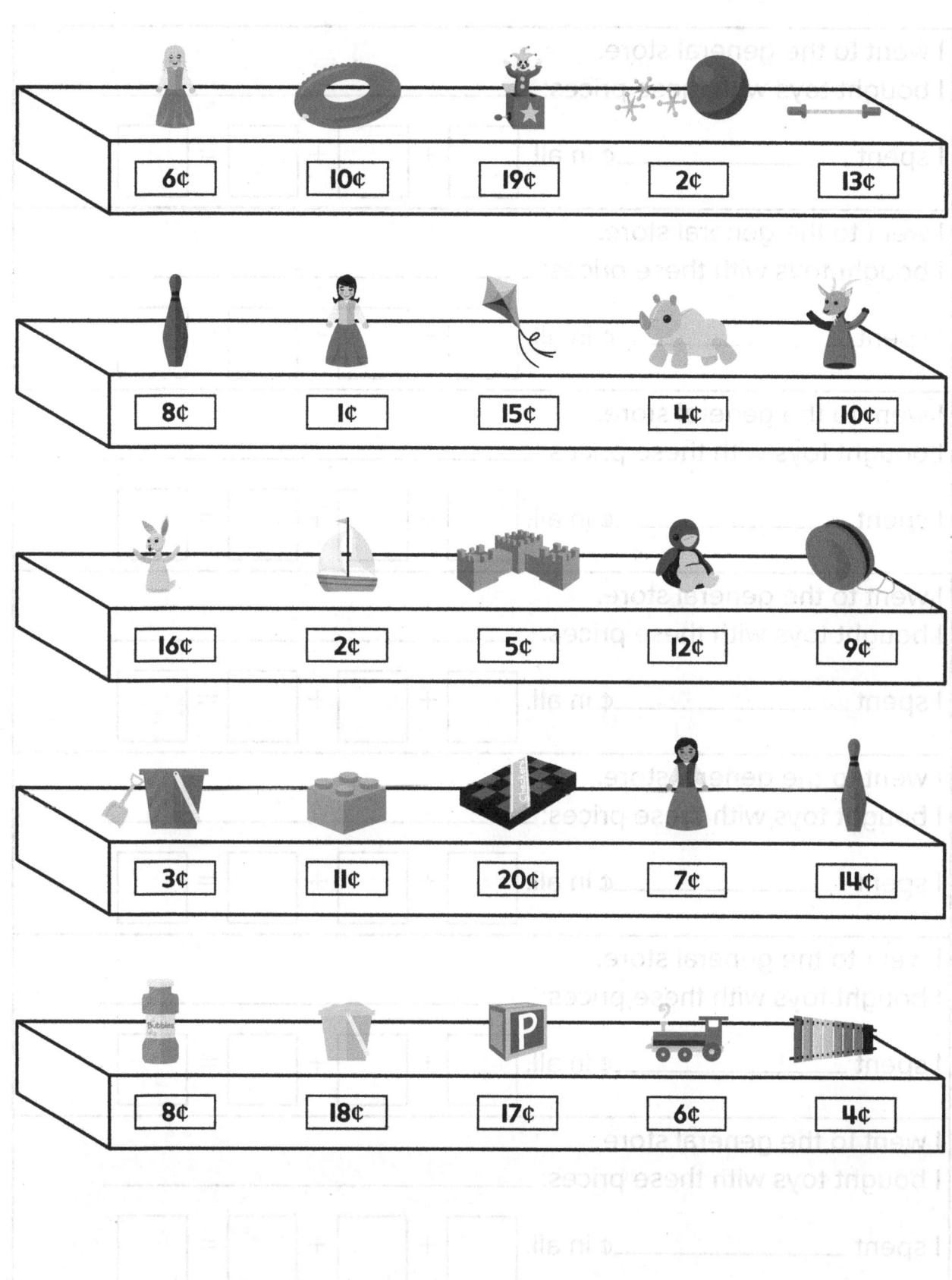

Going Shopping Record Sheet

I went to the general store.
I bought toys with these prices: _____.

I spent _____ ¢ in all. ☐ + ☐ + ☐ = ☐

I went to the general store.
I bought toys with these prices: _____.

I spent _____ ¢ in all. ☐ + ☐ + ☐ = ☐

I went to the general store.
I bought toys with these prices: _____.

I spent _____ ¢ in all. ☐ + ☐ + ☐ = ☐

I went to the general store.
I bought toys with these prices: _____.

I spent _____ ¢ in all. ☐ + ☐ + ☐ = ☐

I went to the general store.
I bought toys with these prices: _____.

I spent _____ ¢ in all. ☐ + ☐ + ☐ = ☐

I went to the general store.
I bought toys with these prices: _____.

I spent _____ ¢ in all. ☐ + ☐ + ☐ = ☐

I went to the general store.
I bought toys with these prices: _____.

I spent _____ ¢ in all. ☐ + ☐ + ☐ = ☐

Measuring Record Sheet

1	1	1	1
2	2	2	2
3	3	3	3
4	4	4	4
5	5	5	5
6	6	6	6
7	7	7	7
8	8	8	8
9	9	9	9
10	10	10	10

Shape Outlines

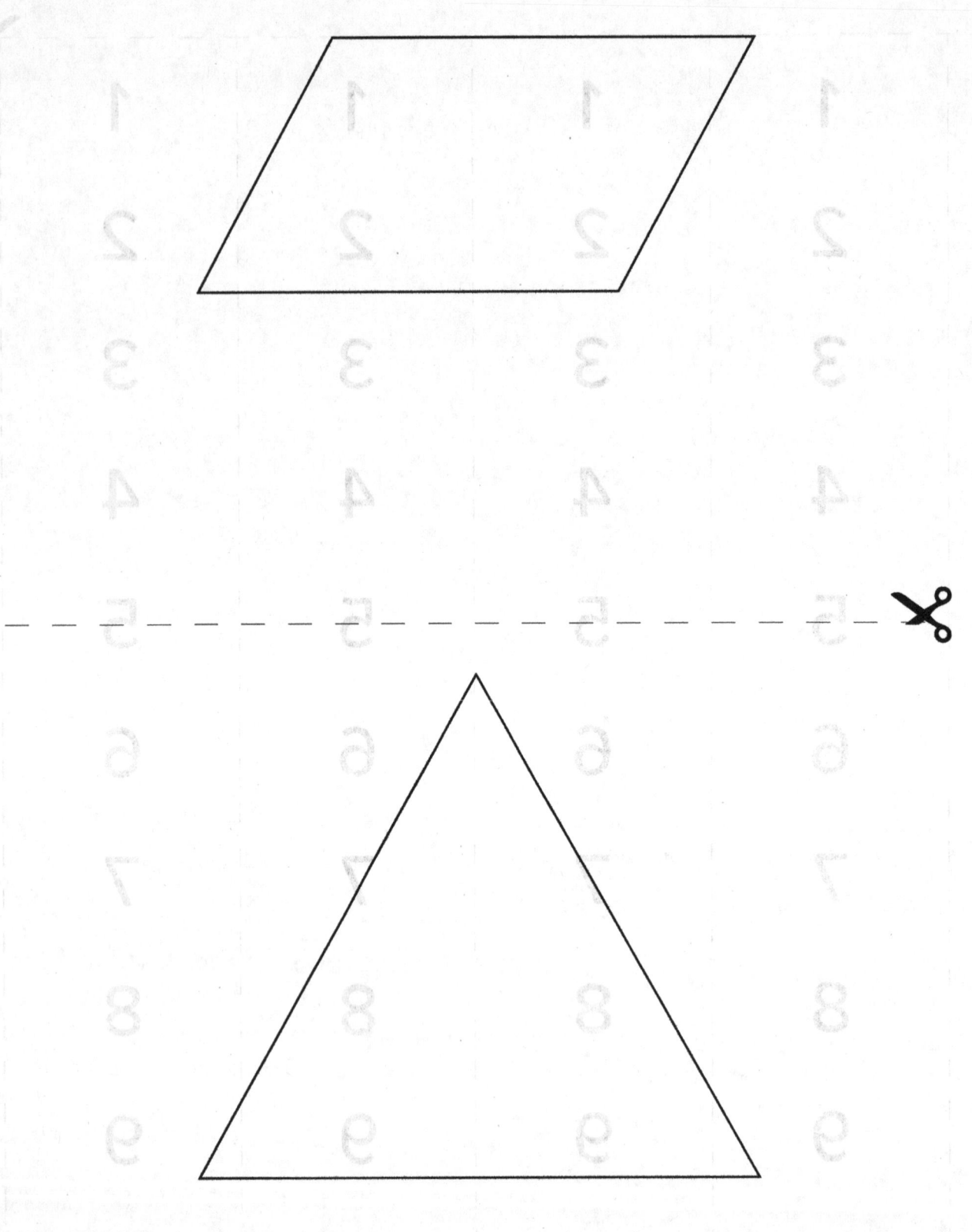

36 Shape Outlines (1 of 3) • **Games Kit Resource Guide**

Shape Outlines

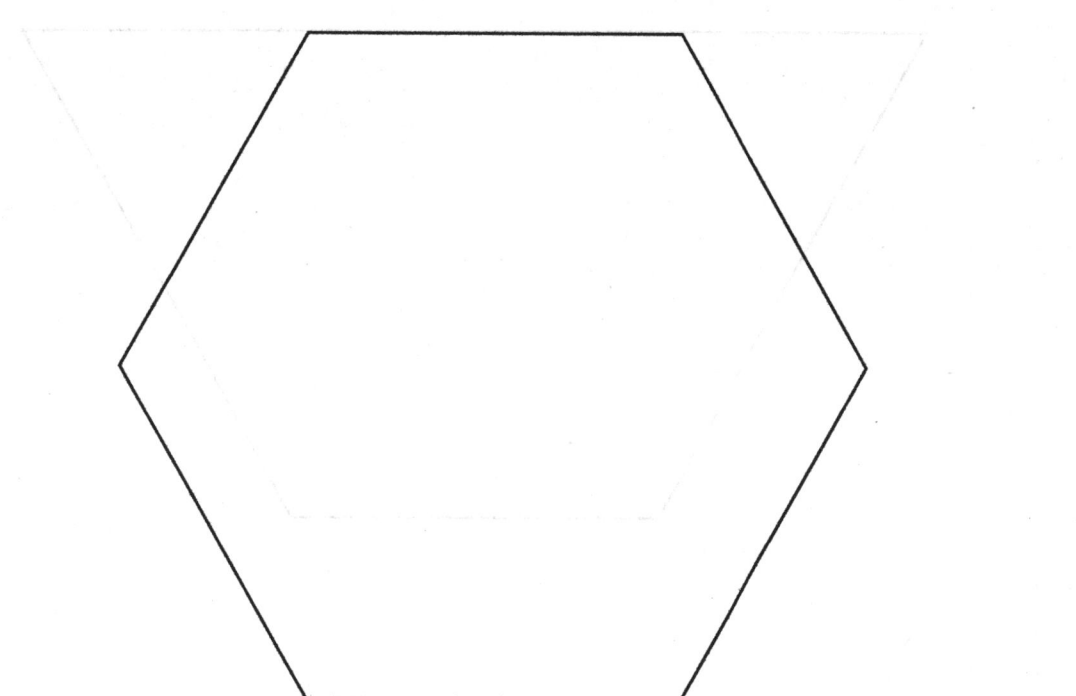

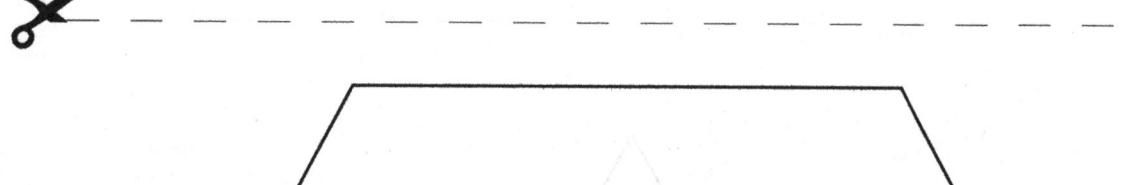

Shape Outlines

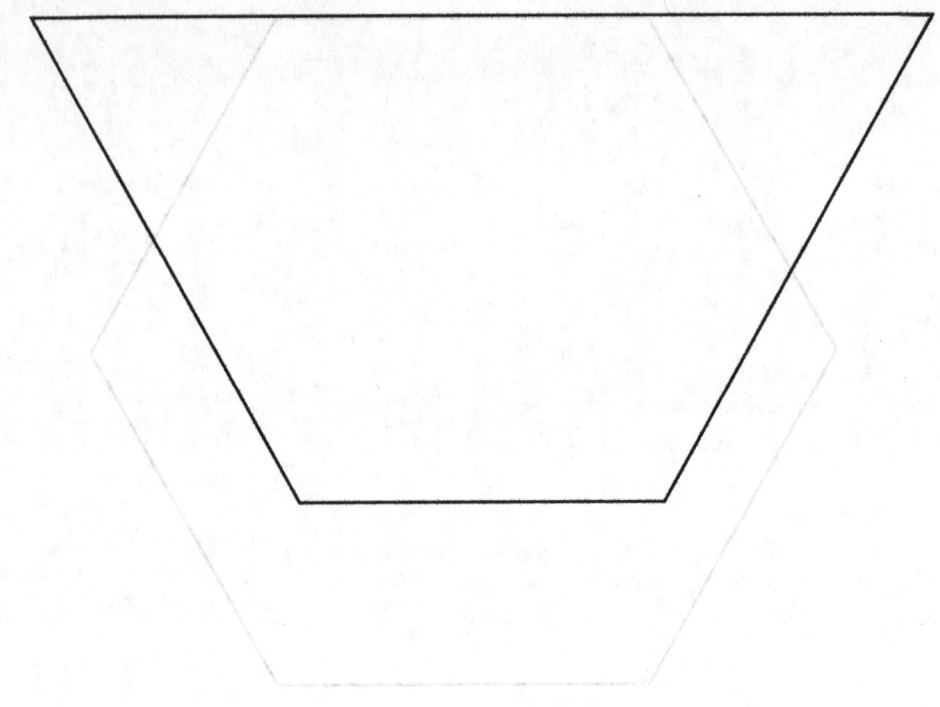

------- ✂

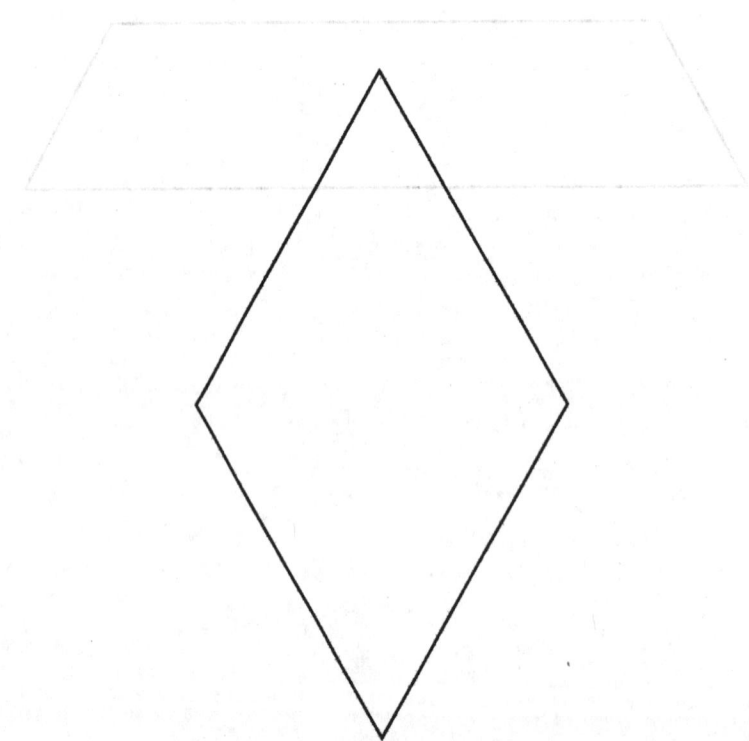

Drop the Counter Bar Graph

In

Out

Games Kit Resource Guide • Drop the Counter Bar Graph

Here I Come! Construction Mat

Hundreds	Tens	Ones

Equation Record Sheet

Example: 35 − 31 = 4
          4 + 35 = 39

---

35 ◯ ☐ = ☐

☐ ◯ ☐ = ☐

☐ ◯ ☐ = ☐

☐ ◯ ☐ = ☐

☐ ◯ ☐ = ☐

☐ ◯ ☐ = ☐

☐ ◯ ☐ = ☐

☐ ◯ ☐ = ☐

☐ ◯ ☐ = ☐

☐ ◯ ☐ = ☐

☐ ◯ ☐ = ☐

Gopher It! Record Sheet

Example:
My gopher started at __5__.
It moved __3__ spaces backward.
It is now at __2__.

My gopher started at ____. It moved ____ spaces _____ward. It is now at ____.	My gopher started at ____. It moved ____ spaces _____ward. It is now at ____.
My gopher started at ____. It moved ____ spaces _____ward. It is now at ____.	My gopher started at ____. It moved ____ spaces _____ward. It is now at ____.
My gopher started at ____. It moved ____ spaces _____ward. It is now at ____.	My gopher started at ____. It moved ____ spaces _____ward. It is now at ____.

Measurement Hunt Record Sheet

Measurement Number	Measurement in Inches
Measurement 1	
Measurement 2	
Measurement 3	
Measurement 4	
Measurement 5	
Measurement 6	
Measurement 7	
Measurement 8	

- ✂

Measurement Number	Measurement in Inches
Measurement 1	
Measurement 2	
Measurement 3	
Measurement 4	
Measurement 5	
Measurement 6	
Measurement 7	
Measurement 8	

Blank Bingo Mat

Shape Bingo Cards

exactly 3 sides	exactly 4 sides	exactly 5 sides	exactly 6 sides
exactly 3 angles	exactly 4 angles	exactly 5 angles	exactly 6 angles
all sides equal	all sides equal	exactly 4 angles	2 sides the same
exactly 3 sides	exactly 4 sides	exactly 5 sides	exactly 6 sides
6 equal faces	no sides equal	no sides equal	exactly 4 angles

Shape Bingo Mat

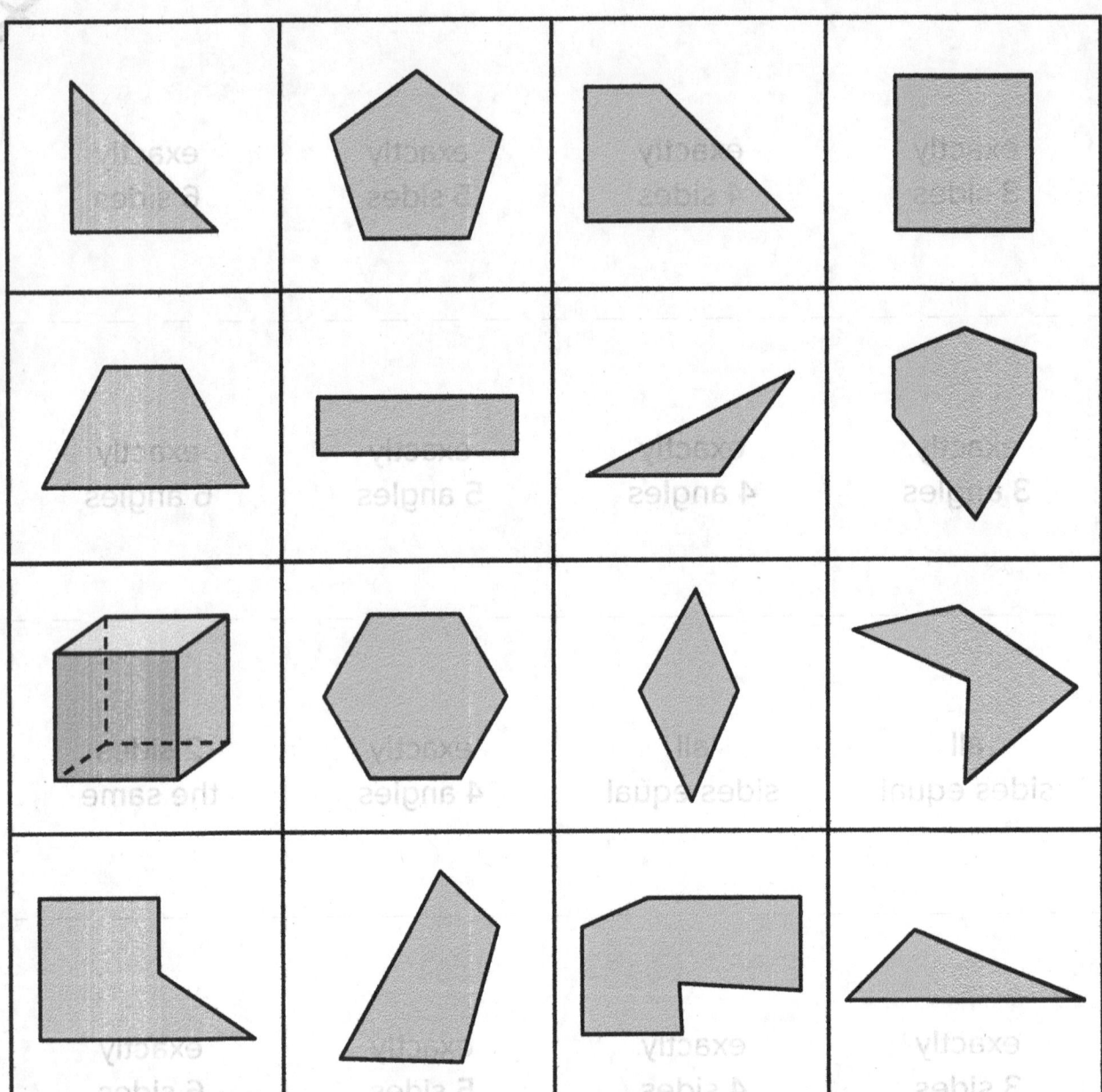

46 Shape Bingo Mat (1 of 4) • Games Kit Resource Guide

Shape Bingo Mat

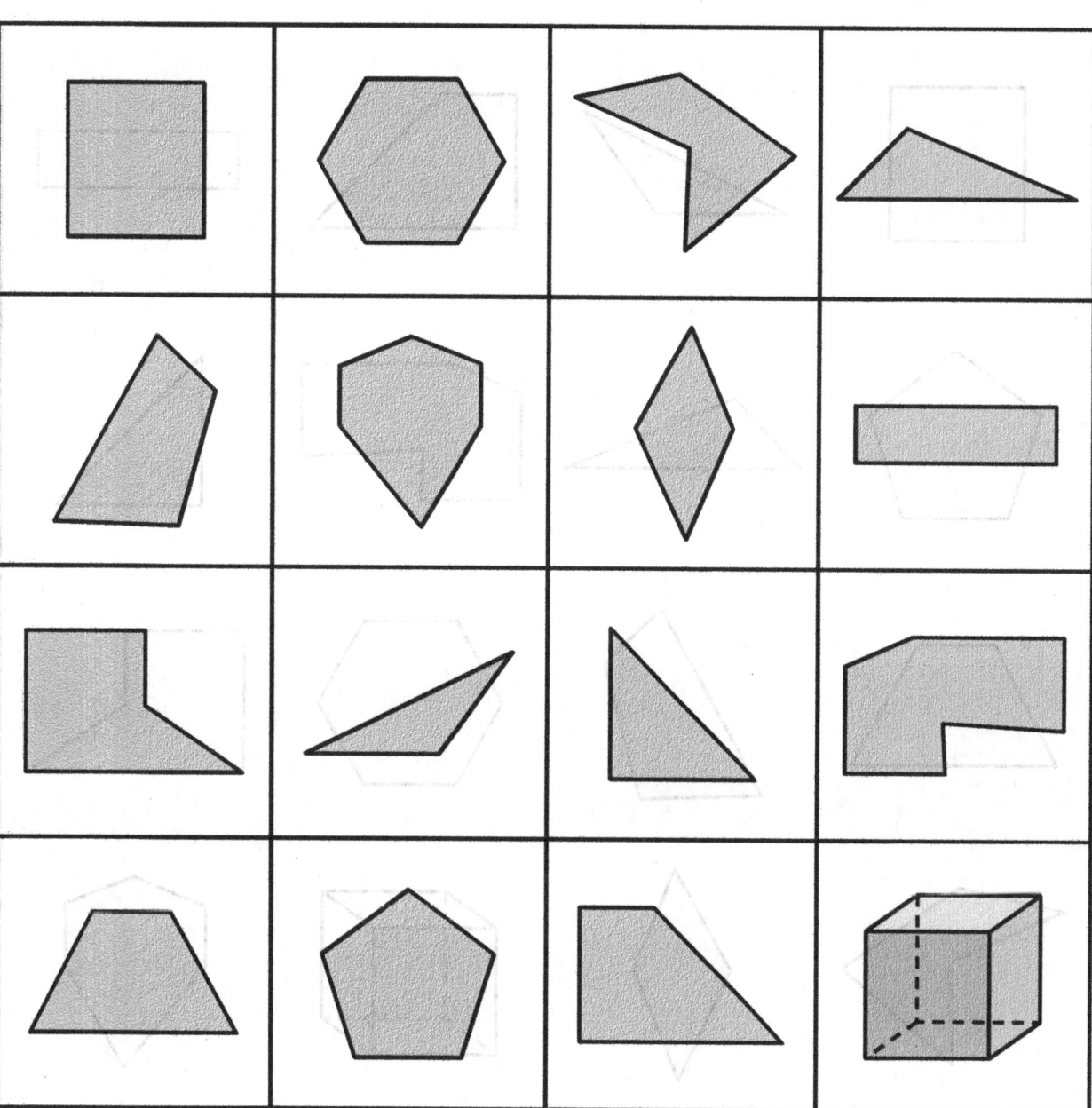

Shape Bingo Mat

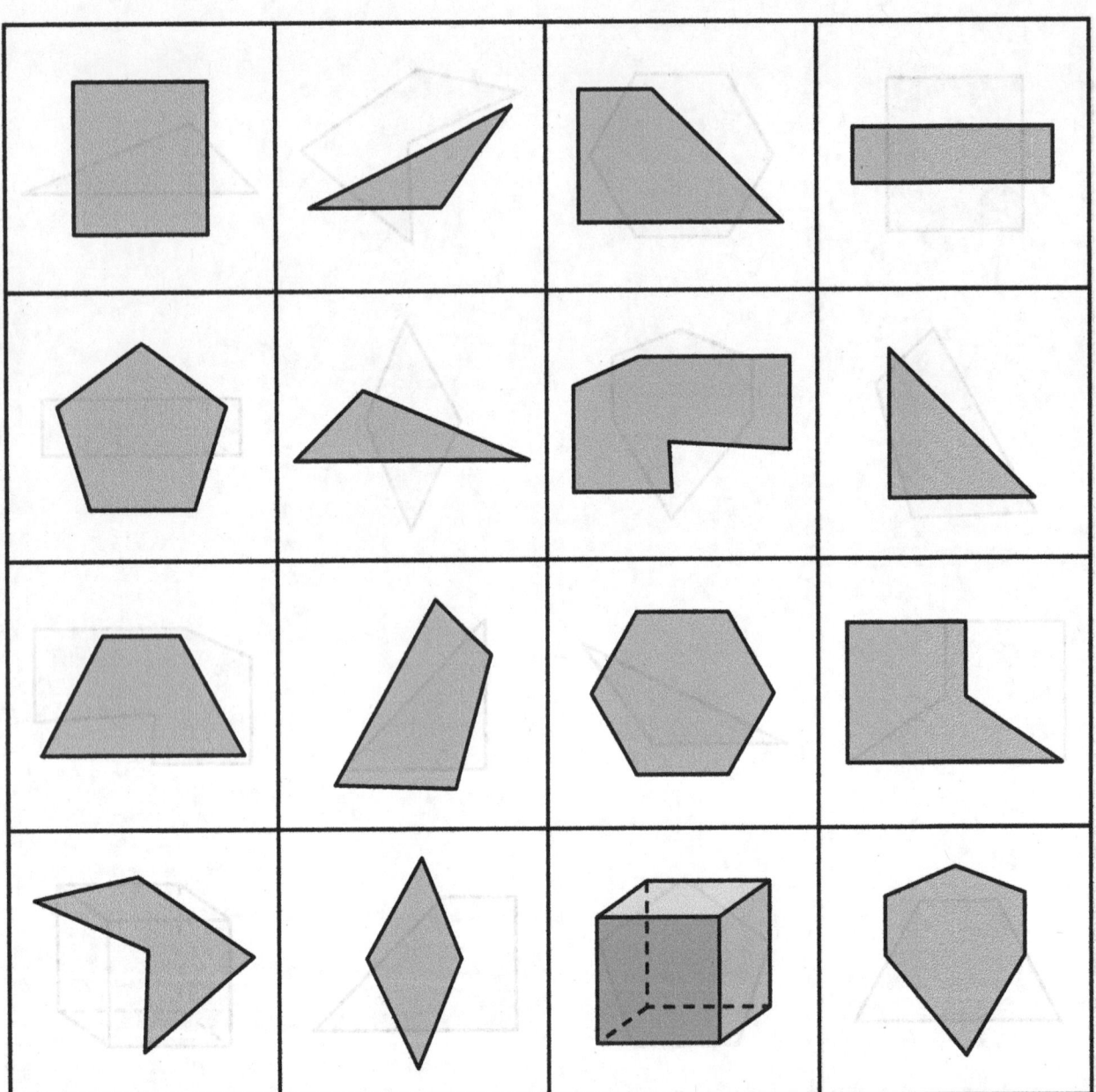

Shape Bingo Mat

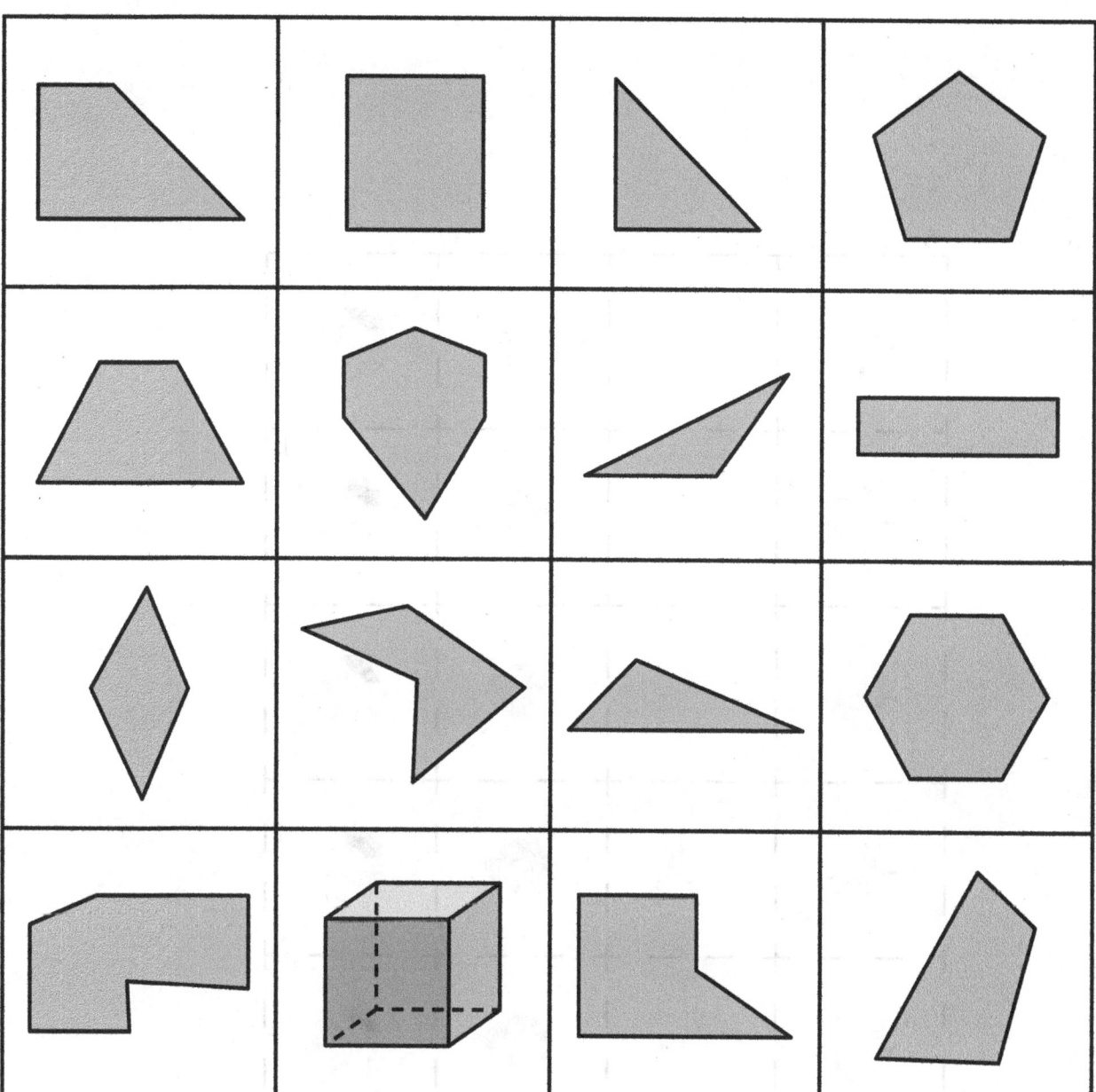

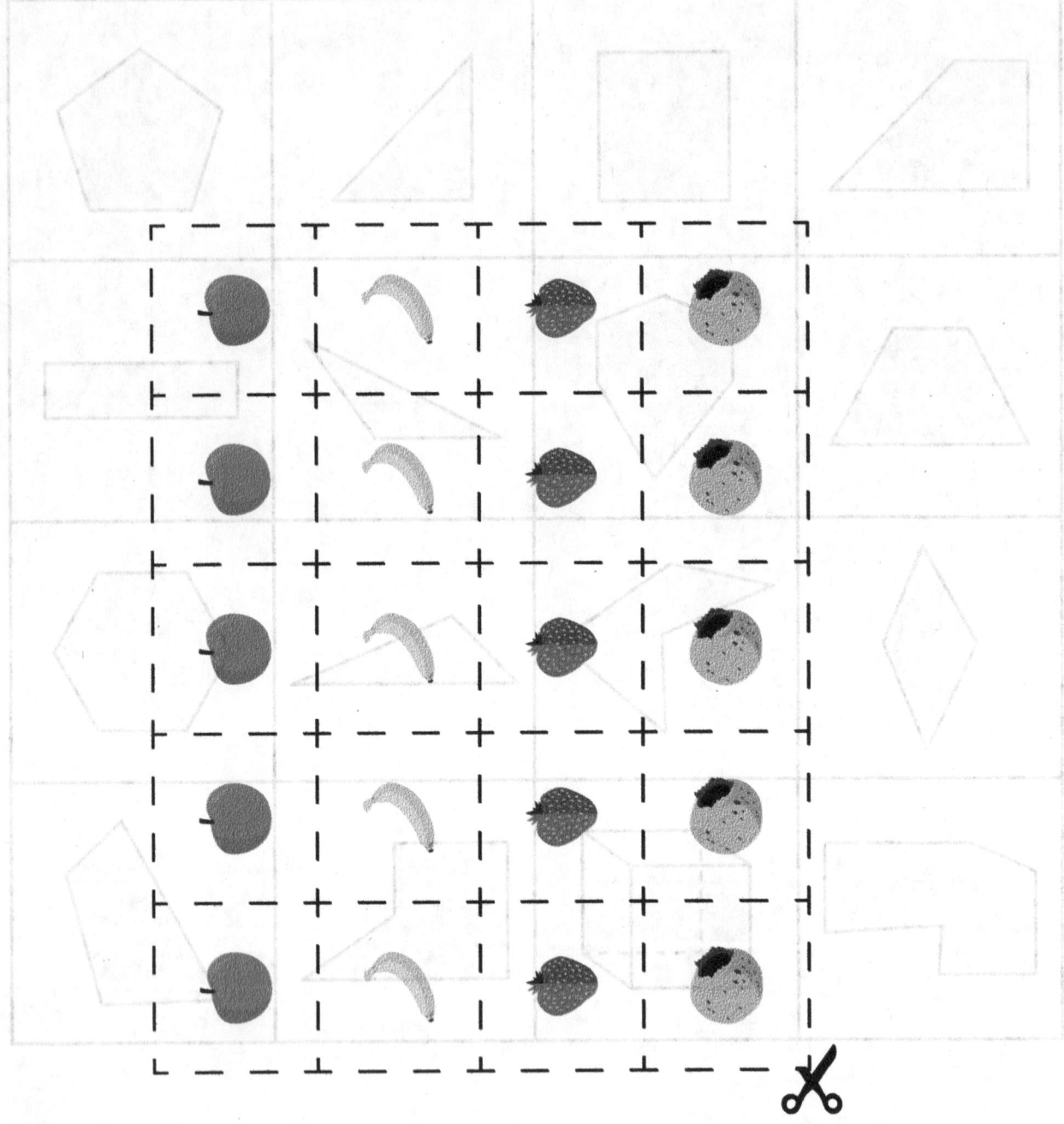

Fruit Cards

50 Fruit Cards • **Games Kit Resource Guide**

Fruit Collector Bar Graph

Fruit Collected

Number of Fruits

8
7
6
5
4
3
2
1
0

Apple   Banana   Strawberry   Blueberry

Fruit

Fruit Collector Picture Graph

Fruit Collected

Apple	Banana	Strawberry	Blueberry

Each picture = 1 Fruit

52 Fruit Collector Picture Graph • **Games Kit Resource Guide**

Fruit Collector Question Cards

What is the total number of fruit?	What is the total number of fruit?
How many apples and blueberries do you have in all?	How many strawberries and bananas do you have in all?
Which has more: apples or blueberries? How many more?	Which has more: bananas or blueberries? How many more?
What is the total number of fruit?	What is the total number of fruit?
How many apples and bananas do you have in all?	How many blueberries and strawberries do you have in all?
Which has more: apples or strawberries? How many more?	Which has more: apples or blueberries? How many more?

Multiplication Table

×	0	1	2	3	4	5	6	7	8	9	10
0	0	0	0	0	0	0	0	0	0	0	0
1	0	1	2	3	4	5	6	7	8	9	10
2	0	2	4	6	8	10	12	14	16	18	20
3	0	3	6	9	12	15	18	21	24	27	30
4	0	4	8	12	16	20	24	28	32	36	40
5	0	5	10	15	20	25	30	35	40	45	50
6	0	6	12	18	24	30	36	42	48	54	60
7	0	7	14	21	28	35	42	49	56	63	70
8	0	8	16	24	32	40	48	56	64	72	80
9	0	9	18	27	36	45	54	63	72	81	90
10	0	10	20	30	40	50	60	70	80	90	100

Riddle Cards

Joe has 7 buckets of 9 apples. He has 63 apples. Sam has 9 buckets of 7 apples. How many apples does Sam have? How do you know?

Beth has 5 bins with no basketballs in them. How many basketballs does Beth have in the bins all together? Why?

Dave is hosting a party for 10 friends. How many party hats should he buy so that everyone has a hat? Why?

Al has 3 bins of 4 toys. Lee has 4 bins of 3 toys. Lee says he has more toys. Is he right? Why or why not?

Kay is reading out products of a factor. She reads, "9, 12, 15, 18, 21." What is the factor? How do you know?

What do you notice about all of the products with a factor of 10?

What do you notice about all of the products with a factor of 4?

What do you notice about all of the products with a factor of 2?

What is special about the products on the diagonal of the multiplication table? (To help you figure this out, draw a line from the × to 100.)

What do you notice about all of the products of 9?

Look at the row for the products of 4. Look at the row for the products of 8. How are they related?

What do you notice about the products in rows 2, 4, 6, 8, and 10 of the multiplication table?

Riddle Cards

Ann has 5 plates of 4 berries. She has 20 berries. Jeff has 4 plates of 5 berries. How many berries does Jeff have? How do you know?

Addie has 8 dollhouses with no dolls in any of them. How many dolls does Addie have in the dollhouses? How do you know?

Nate is hosting a party for 5 friends. How many balloons should he buy so everyone has 1 balloon? Why?

James has 6 boxes of 8 sweaters. Zack has 8 boxes of 6 sweaters. Zack says he has more sweaters. Is he right? Why or why not?

Tom is reading out some products of a factor. He reads, "20, 25, 30, 35, 40." What is the factor? How do you know?

Tina is reading out some products of a factor. She reads, "12, 18, 24, 30." What is the factor? How do you know?

Look at the row for the products of 2. Look at the row for the products of 6. How are they related?

What do you notice about all of the products with a factor of 0?

Look at where row 2 and column 5 meet. Look at where row 5 and column 2 meet. What do you notice?

Why is the first column of the multiplication table all zeros?

Look at the row for products of 5. Look at the row for products of 10. How are they related?

What do you notice about all of the products with a factor of 5?

Master Builder Cards

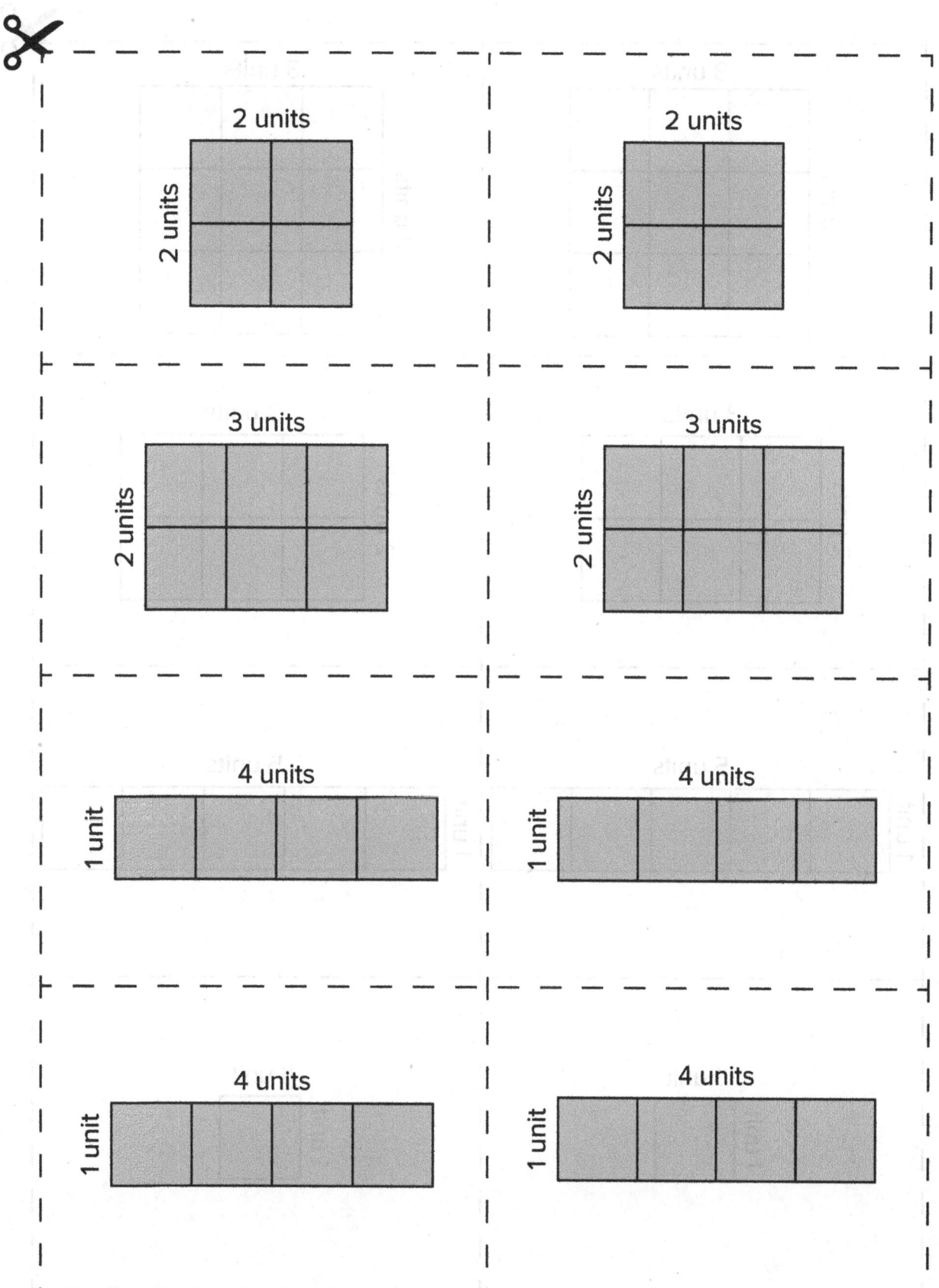

Master Builder Cards

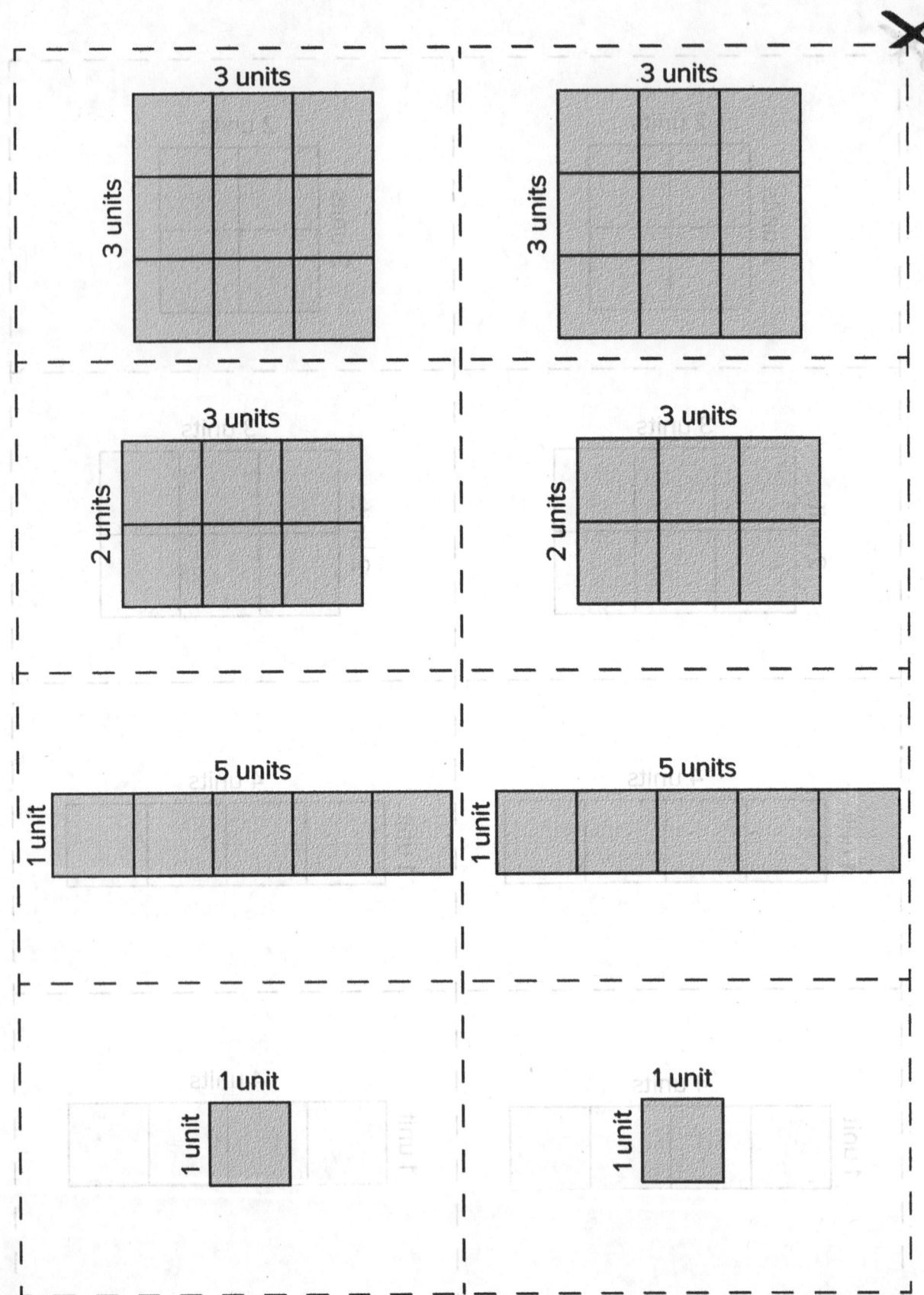

Attribute Cards

4 sides of equal lengths	2 pairs of sides of equal lengths	no sides of equal lengths
1 pair of parallel sides	2 pairs of parallel sides	4 square corners
no square corners	4 sides of equal lengths and no square corners	2 pairs of parallel sides and no square corners
4 square corners	2 pairs of sides of equal lengths and no square corners	no parallel sides

Games Kit Resource Guide • Attribute Cards 59

Quadrilateral Guides

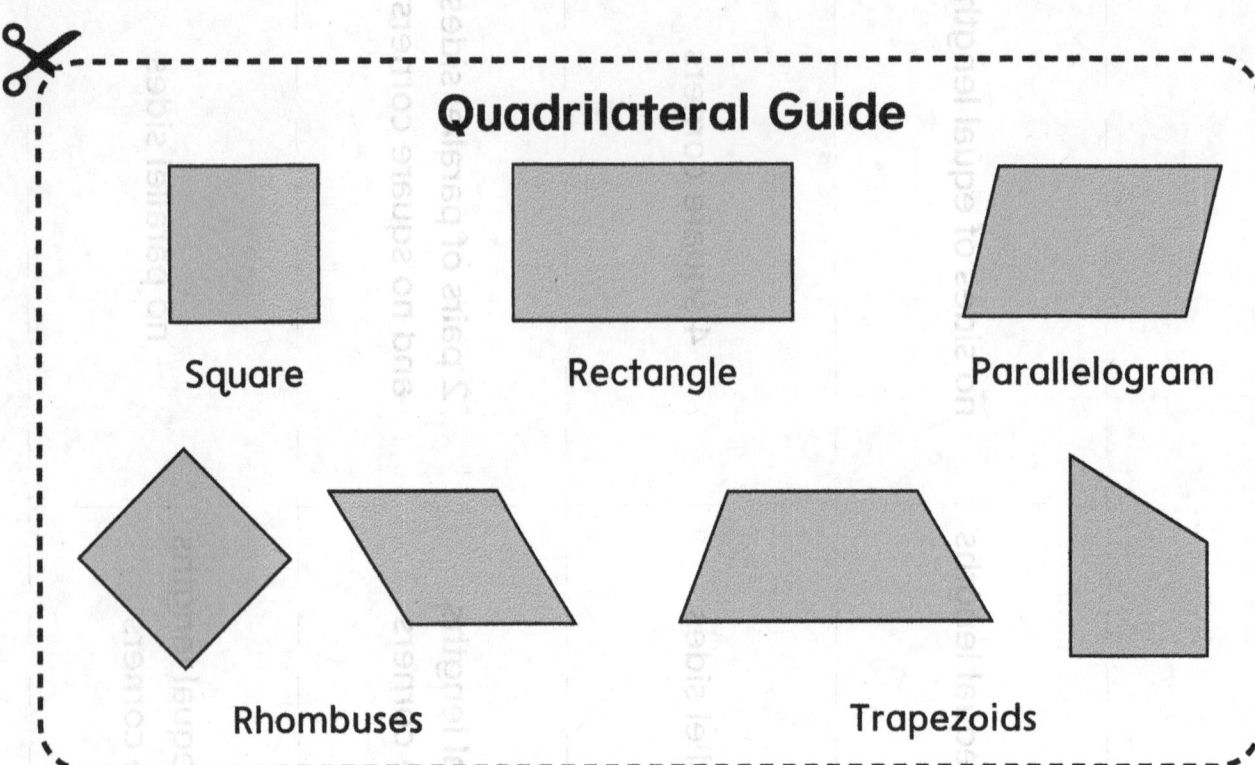

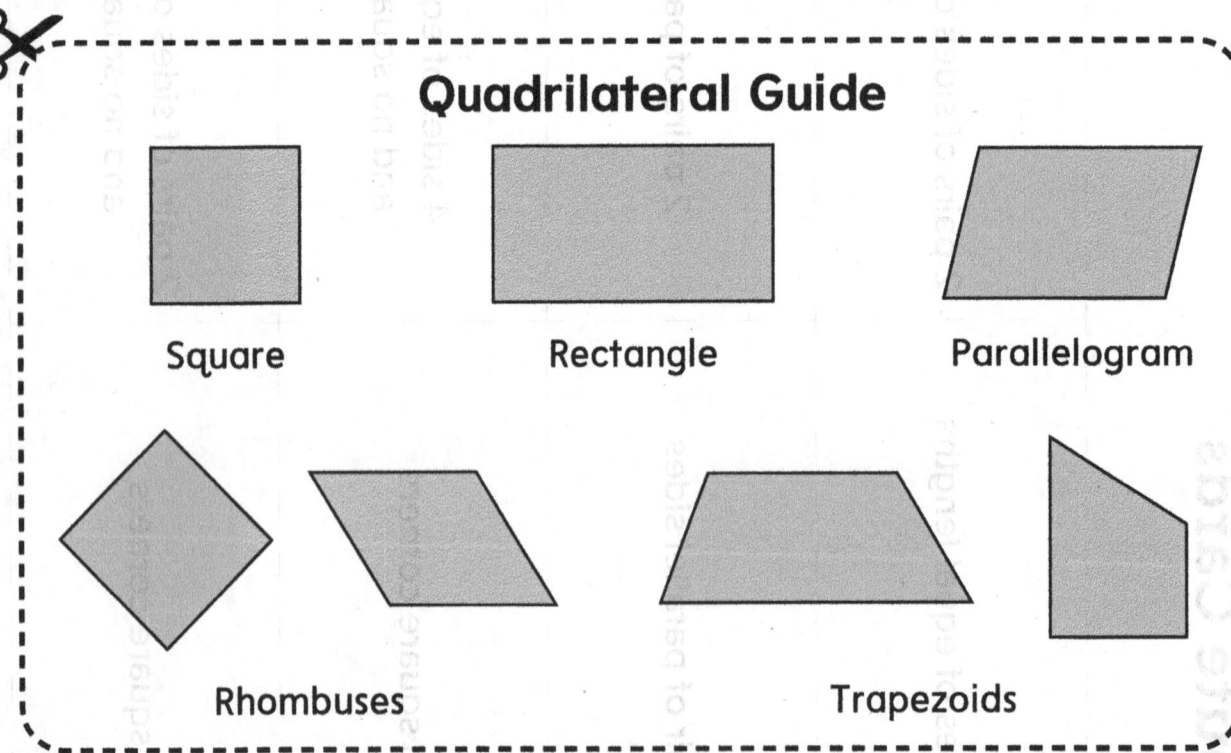

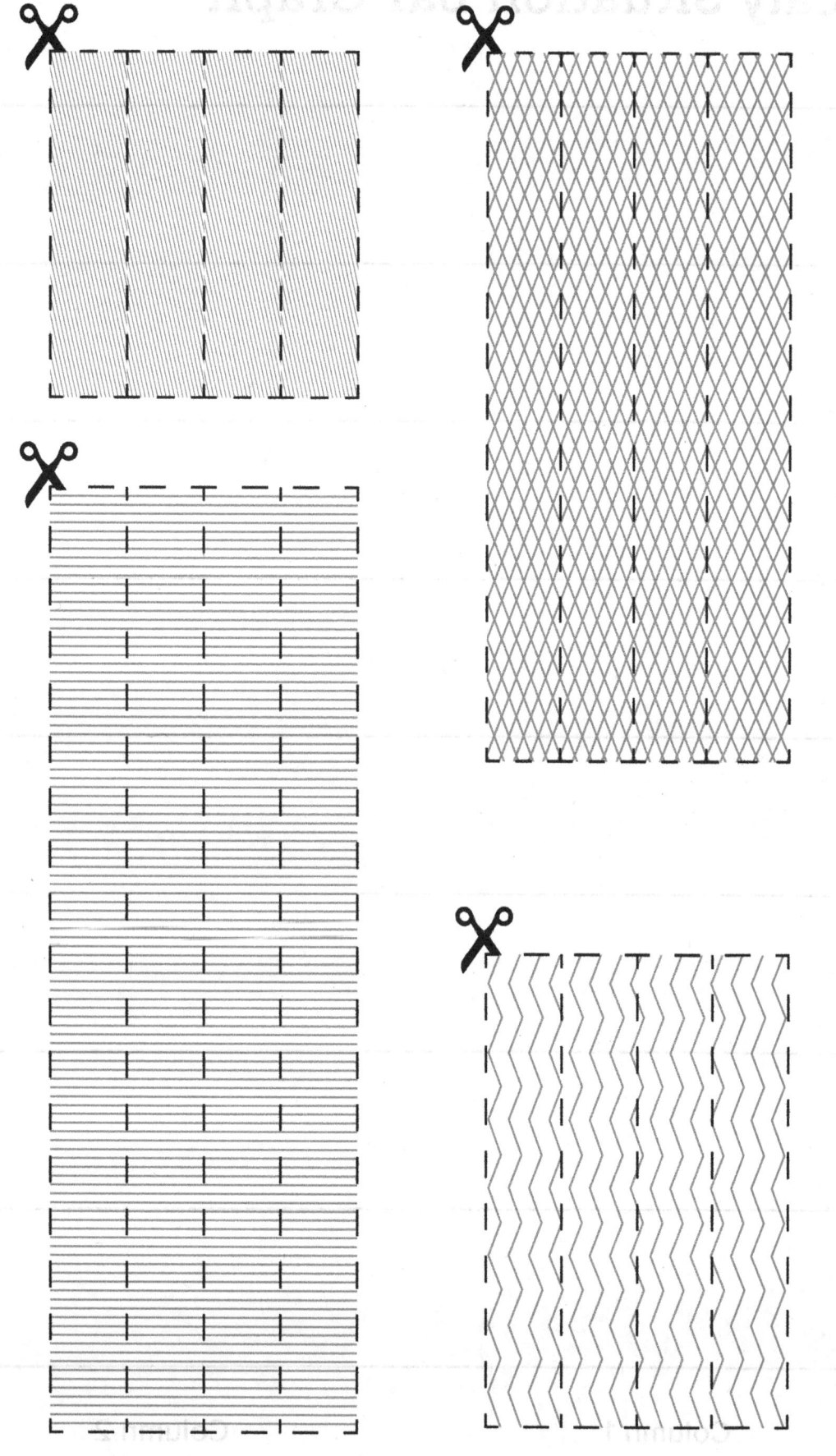

Side Lengths

Games Kit Resource Guide • Side Lengths 61

A Scaly Situation Bar Graph

Column 1   Column 2

62   A Scaly Situation Bar Graph • **Games Kit Resource Guide**

A Scaly Situation Record Sheet

Scale Factor (number on spinner)	Column 1 Value (number of tiles × scale factor)	Column 2 Value (number of tiles × scale factor)	Answer to Word Problem

Word Problem Cards

Emma and Jess have some pets.
Emma's number is in column 1.
Jess' number is in column 2.
How many pets do they have in all?

Greg and Alex collect some cards.
Greg's number is in column 1.
Alex's number is in column 2.
Who has more cards?
How many more?

Mark and Josh baked some rolls.
Mark's number is in column 1.
Josh's number is in column 2.
How many rolls did they bake in all?

May and Sam ate some grapes.
May's number is in column 1.
Sam's number is in column 2.
Who ate more grapes?
How many more?

The man has dogs and cats.
Column 1 is the number of dogs.
Column 2 is the number of cats.
How many dogs and cats does he have in all?

The girl has fish and birds.
Column 1 is the number of fish.
Column 2 is the number of birds.
Does she have more fish or birds?
How many more?

The team has girls and boys.
Column 1 is the number of boys.
Column 2 is the number of girls.
How many players are on the team?

The club has girls and boys.
Column 1 is the number of boys.
Column 2 is the number of girls.
Are there more boys or girls?
How many more?

Word Problem Cards

Jen and Chan collected some cans.
Jen's number is in column 1.
Chan's number is in column 2.
How many cans did they collect in all?

Pete and Meg picked some apples.
Pete's number is in column 1.
Megan's number is in column 2.
Who picked fewer apples?
How many fewer?

Beth and Mac drew some pictures.
Beth's number is in column 1.
Mac's number is in column 2.
How many pictures did they draw in all?

Tom and Jim scored some points.
Tom's number is in column 1.
Jim's number is in column 2.
Who scored fewer points?
How many fewer?

Ann and Chad worked some hours.
Ann's number is in column 1.
Chad's number is in column 2.
How many hours did they work in all?

Sam and Jen built some models.
Sam's number is in column 1.
Jen's number is in column 2.
Who built fewer models?
How many fewer?

Lee and Kay scored some points.
Lee's number is in column 1.
Kay's number is in column 2.
How many points did they score in all?

Ben and Addy fixed some toys.
Ben's number is in column 1.
Addy's number is in column 2.
Who fixed the most toys?
How many more?

Fraction Adding Cards

$\dfrac{1}{4}+\dfrac{2}{4}$	$\dfrac{1}{5}+\dfrac{3}{5}$
$\dfrac{1}{4}+\dfrac{1}{4}$	$\dfrac{1}{5}+\dfrac{2}{5}$
$\dfrac{1}{3}+\dfrac{2}{3}$	$\dfrac{1}{5}+\dfrac{1}{5}$
$\dfrac{1}{3}+\dfrac{1}{3}$	$\dfrac{2}{4}+\dfrac{2}{4}$
$\dfrac{1}{2}+\dfrac{1}{2}$	$\dfrac{3}{4}+\dfrac{1}{4}$

Fraction Adding Cards

$\dfrac{1}{6}+\dfrac{2}{6}$　　$\dfrac{3}{6}+\dfrac{2}{6}$

$\dfrac{1}{6}+\dfrac{1}{6}$　　$\dfrac{2}{6}+\dfrac{2}{6}$

$\dfrac{2}{5}+\dfrac{2}{5}$　　$\dfrac{1}{6}+\dfrac{5}{6}$

$\dfrac{2}{5}+\dfrac{3}{5}$　　$\dfrac{4}{6}+\dfrac{1}{6}$

$\dfrac{4}{5}+\dfrac{1}{5}$　　$\dfrac{1}{6}+\dfrac{3}{6}$

Fraction Adding Cards

$\frac{6}{8}+\frac{1}{8}$	$\frac{5}{8}+\frac{3}{8}$
$\frac{1}{8}+\frac{4}{8}$	$\frac{3}{8}+\frac{4}{8}$
$\frac{1}{8}+\frac{2}{8}$	$\frac{2}{8}+\frac{5}{8}$
$\frac{1}{8}+\frac{1}{8}$	$\frac{4}{8}+\frac{2}{8}$
$\frac{2}{6}+\frac{4}{6}$	$\frac{2}{8}+\frac{3}{8}$

Fraction Adding Cards

$\dfrac{4}{12} + \dfrac{2}{12}$

$\dfrac{9}{12} + \dfrac{2}{12}$

$\dfrac{1}{12} + \dfrac{10}{12}$

$\dfrac{3}{12} + \dfrac{6}{12}$

$\dfrac{7}{12} + \dfrac{1}{12}$

$\dfrac{4}{12} + \dfrac{7}{12}$

$\dfrac{1}{12} + \dfrac{4}{12}$

$\dfrac{5}{12} + \dfrac{3}{12}$

$\dfrac{1}{12} + \dfrac{1}{12}$

$\dfrac{2}{12} + \dfrac{5}{12}$

Fraction Subtracting Cards

$\dfrac{4}{4} - \dfrac{2}{4}$	$\dfrac{5}{5} - \dfrac{3}{5}$
$\dfrac{4}{4} - \dfrac{1}{4}$	$\dfrac{4}{5} - \dfrac{2}{5}$
$\dfrac{3}{3} - \dfrac{2}{3}$	$\dfrac{5}{5} - \dfrac{1}{5}$
$\dfrac{3}{3} - \dfrac{1}{3}$	$\dfrac{2}{4} - \dfrac{2}{4}$
$\dfrac{2}{2} - \dfrac{1}{2}$	$\dfrac{3}{4} - \dfrac{1}{4}$

Fraction Subtracting Cards

$\dfrac{6}{6} - \dfrac{2}{6}$	$\dfrac{3}{6} - \dfrac{2}{6}$
$\dfrac{6}{6} - \dfrac{1}{6}$	$\dfrac{2}{6} - \dfrac{2}{6}$
$\dfrac{4}{5} - \dfrac{1}{5}$	$\dfrac{5}{6} - \dfrac{1}{6}$
$\dfrac{3}{5} - \dfrac{2}{5}$	$\dfrac{5}{6} - \dfrac{2}{6}$
$\dfrac{5}{5} - \dfrac{4}{5}$	$\dfrac{6}{6} - \dfrac{3}{6}$

Fraction Subtracting Cards

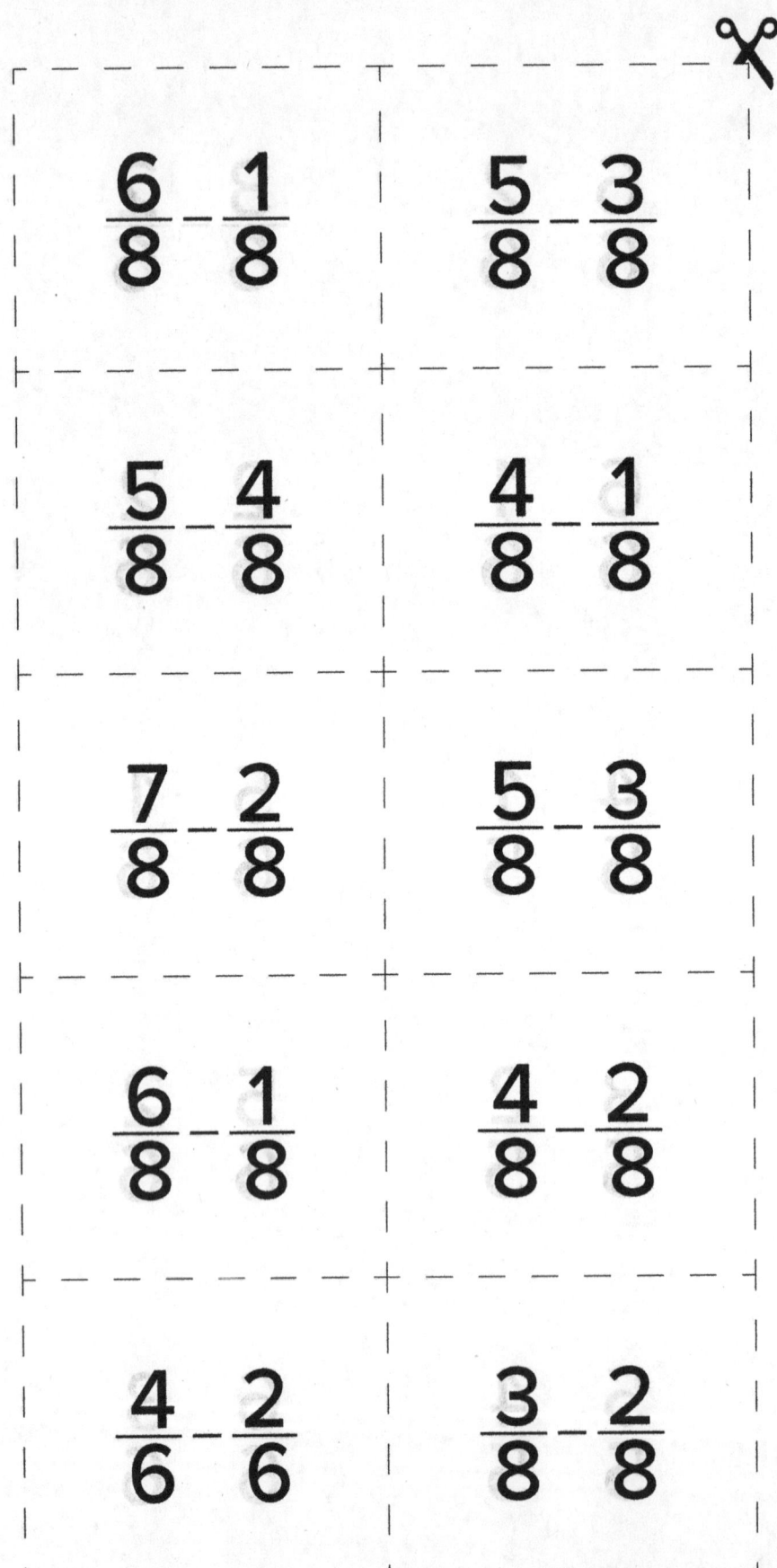

Fraction Subtracting Cards

$\dfrac{4}{12} - \dfrac{2}{12}$	$\dfrac{9}{12} - \dfrac{2}{12}$
$\dfrac{10}{12} - \dfrac{1}{12}$	$\dfrac{6}{12} - \dfrac{3}{12}$
$\dfrac{7}{12} - \dfrac{1}{12}$	$\dfrac{7}{12} - \dfrac{4}{12}$
$\dfrac{4}{12} - \dfrac{1}{12}$	$\dfrac{5}{12} - \dfrac{3}{12}$
$\dfrac{11}{12} - \dfrac{1}{12}$	$\dfrac{10}{12} - \dfrac{5}{12}$

Jumble Cards

1	1	1
2	2	2
3	3	3
5	5	5
6	6	6

Jumble Cards

4	4	4
12	12	12
8	8	8
24	24	24
15	15	15

Jumble Cards

30	30	30
1	1	1
2	2	2
3	3	3
5	5	5

Jumble Cards

6	6	6
4	4	4
2	2	2
3	3	3
4	4	4

Customary Research

How far away from the crash was it found?	How much goo was found?	How much did the goo weigh?	How long ago was the goo found?
_____ in.	_____ fl oz	_____ oz	_____ sec
1 ft = 12 in. 1 yard = 3 feet	1 cup = 8 fl oz 1 pint = 2 cups	1 lb = 16 oz	1 min = 60 sec 1 hour = 60 min

If the goo was found:
- Closer than 50 inches to the crash, the goo is from planet Annic.
- Farther than 50 inches to the crash, the goo is from planet Sotak.

If the goo was found:
- Less than 500 secs ago, the goo is radioactive.
- More than 500 secs ago, the goo will glow-in-the-dark.

If the goo weighed:
- Less than 75 oz, the goo will make you fly!
- More than 75 oz, the goo will make you sink into the ground!

If there was less than 30 fl oz of goo found, the goo is trying to make friends.
If there was more than 30 fl oz of goo found, the goo is trying to take over the planet!

My goo is from planet _____ [planet] and is _____ [radioactive or glow-in-the-dark].

It will make me _____ [fly or sink] and it is trying to _____ [make friends or take over the planet].

Metric Research

How far away from the crash was it found?	How much goo was found?	How much did the goo weigh?	How long ago was the goo found?
____ cm	____ mL	____ g	____ sec
1 m = 100 cm	1 L = 1000 mL	1 kg = 1000 g	1 min = 60 sec 1 hour = 60 min

If the goo was found:
- Closer than 450 cm to the crash, the goo is from planet Annic.
- Farther than 450 cm to the crash, the goo is from planet Sotak.

If the goo was found:
- Less than 500 secs ago, the goo is radioactive.
- More than 500 secs ago, the goo will glow-in-the-dark.

If the goo weighed:
- Less than 4000 g, the goo will make you fly!
- More than 4000 g, the goo will make you sink into the ground!

If there was less than 3000 mL of goo found, the goo is trying to make friends.
If there was more than 3000 mL of goo found, the goo is trying to take over the planet!

My goo is from planet _____ [planet] and is _____ [radioactive or glow-in-the-dark]

It will make me _____ [fly or sink] and it is trying to _____ [make friends or take over the planet]

Games Kit Resource Guide • Metric Research 79

Research Cards

The goo was found 2 hours ago.	The goo weighs 3 kg.	2L of goo were found.
The goo was found 4 hours ago.	The goo weighs 5 kg.	5L of goo were found.
The goo was found 10 minutes ago.	The goo weighs 2 lbs.	2 cups of goo were found.
The goo was found 4 minutes ago.	The goo weighs 5 lbs.	4 pints of goo were found.
The goo was found 10 yards from the crash.	The goo weighs 1 kg.	4L of goo were found.
The goo was found 4 feet from the crash.	The goo weighs 6 kg.	6L of goo were found.

Research Cards

The goo was found 3 meters from the crash.	The goo weighs 3 lbs.	3 cups of goo were found.
The goo was found 5 meters from the crash.	The goo weighs 6 lbs.	2 pints of goo were found.
The goo was found 2 yards from the crash.	The goo was found 7 minutes ago.	The goo weighs 2 kg.
The goo was found 6 feet from the crash.	The goo was found 4 hours ago.	The goo weighs 6 kg.
The goo was found 4 meters from the crash.	The goo was found 6 minutes ago.	The goo weighs 3 lbs.
The goo was found 2 meters from the crash.	The goo was found 5 minutes ago.	The goo weighs 4 lbs.

Attribute Bingo Cards

at least 1 pair of parallel lines	2 pairs of parallel lines	at least 1 pair of perpendicular lines
2 pairs of perpendicular lines	at least 1 right angle	at least 2 right angles
4 right angles	2 acute angles	1 obtuse angle
2 obtuse angles	at least 1 pair of parallel and 1 pair of perpendicular lines	1 right angle and at least 1 obtuse angle
no parallel or perpendicular lines	2 pairs of equal sides	at least 1 pair of equal sides

Blank Shape Mat

S	H	A	P	E

Games Kit Resource Guide • Blank Shape Mat   83

Shape Mat

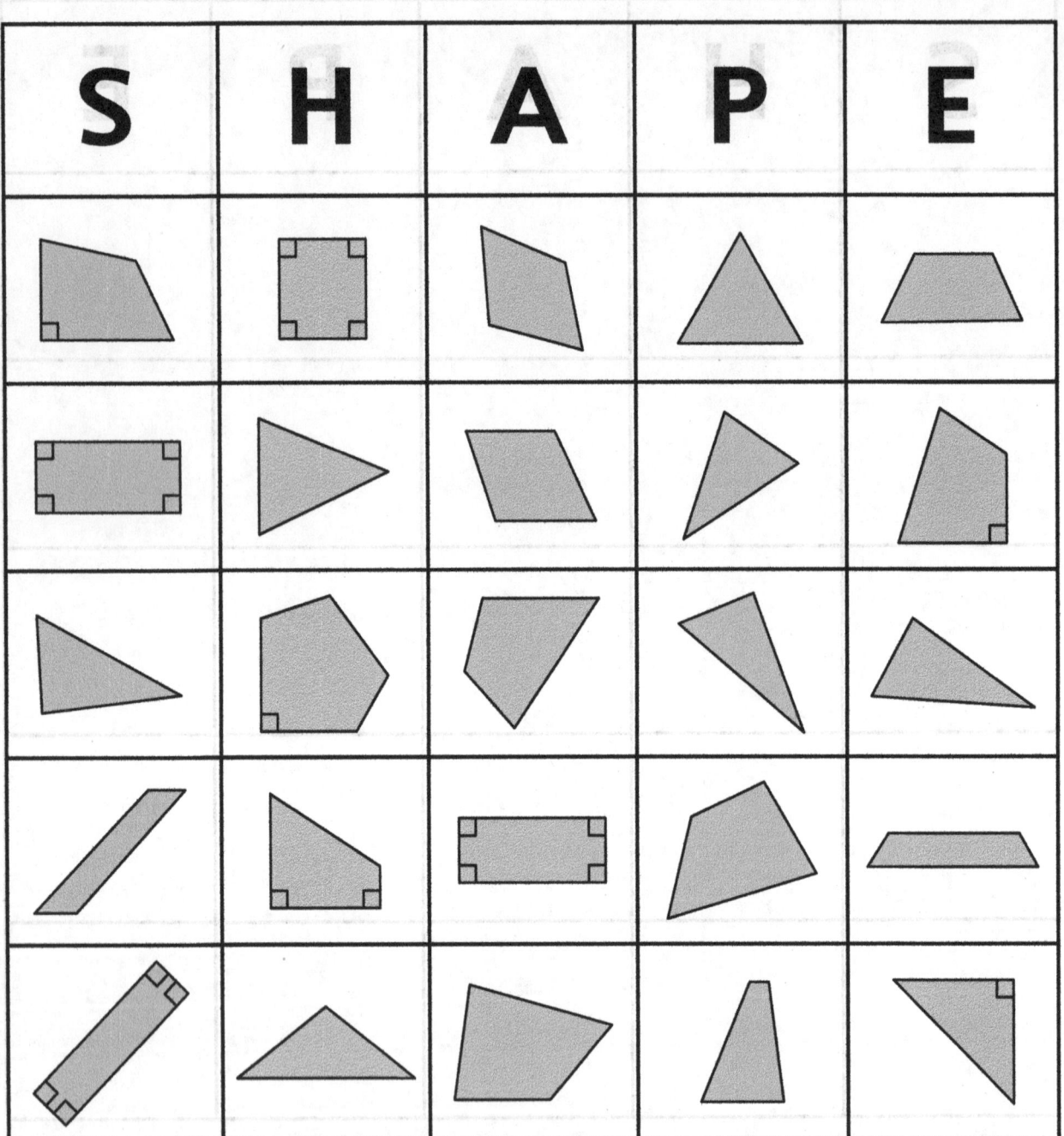

84 Shape Mat (1 of 4) • **Games Kit Resource Guide**

Shape Mat

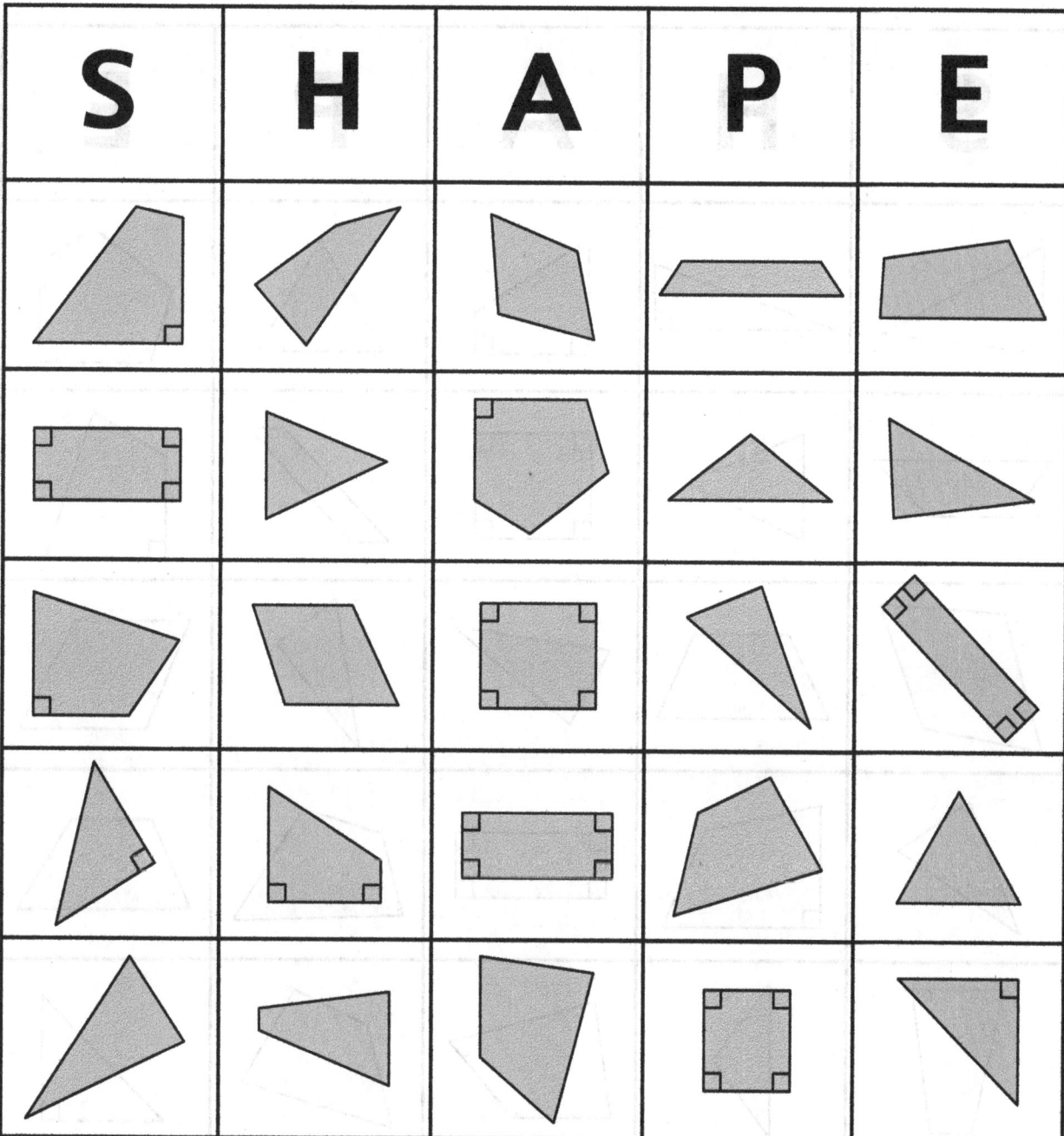

Shape Mat

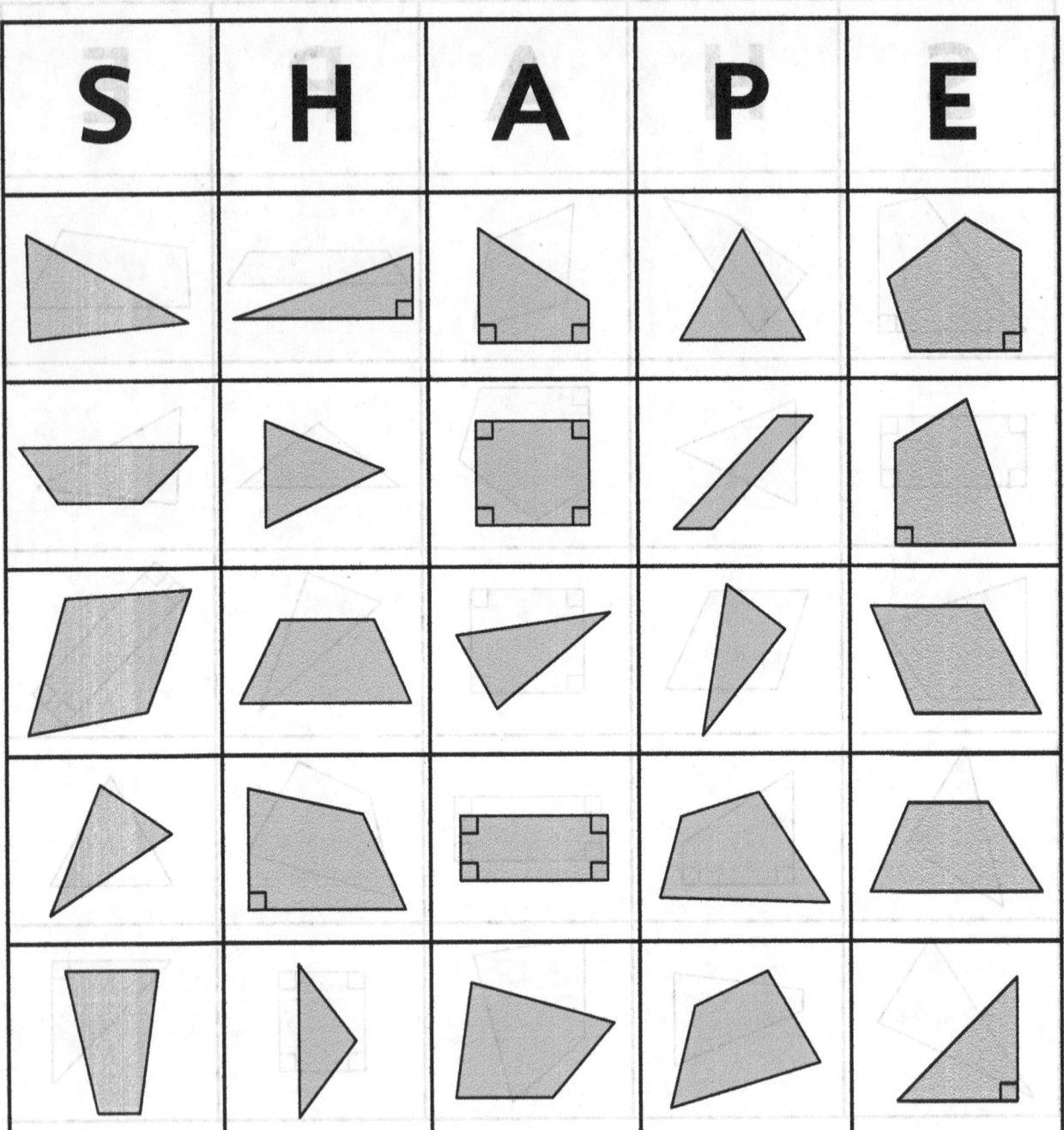

Shape Mat

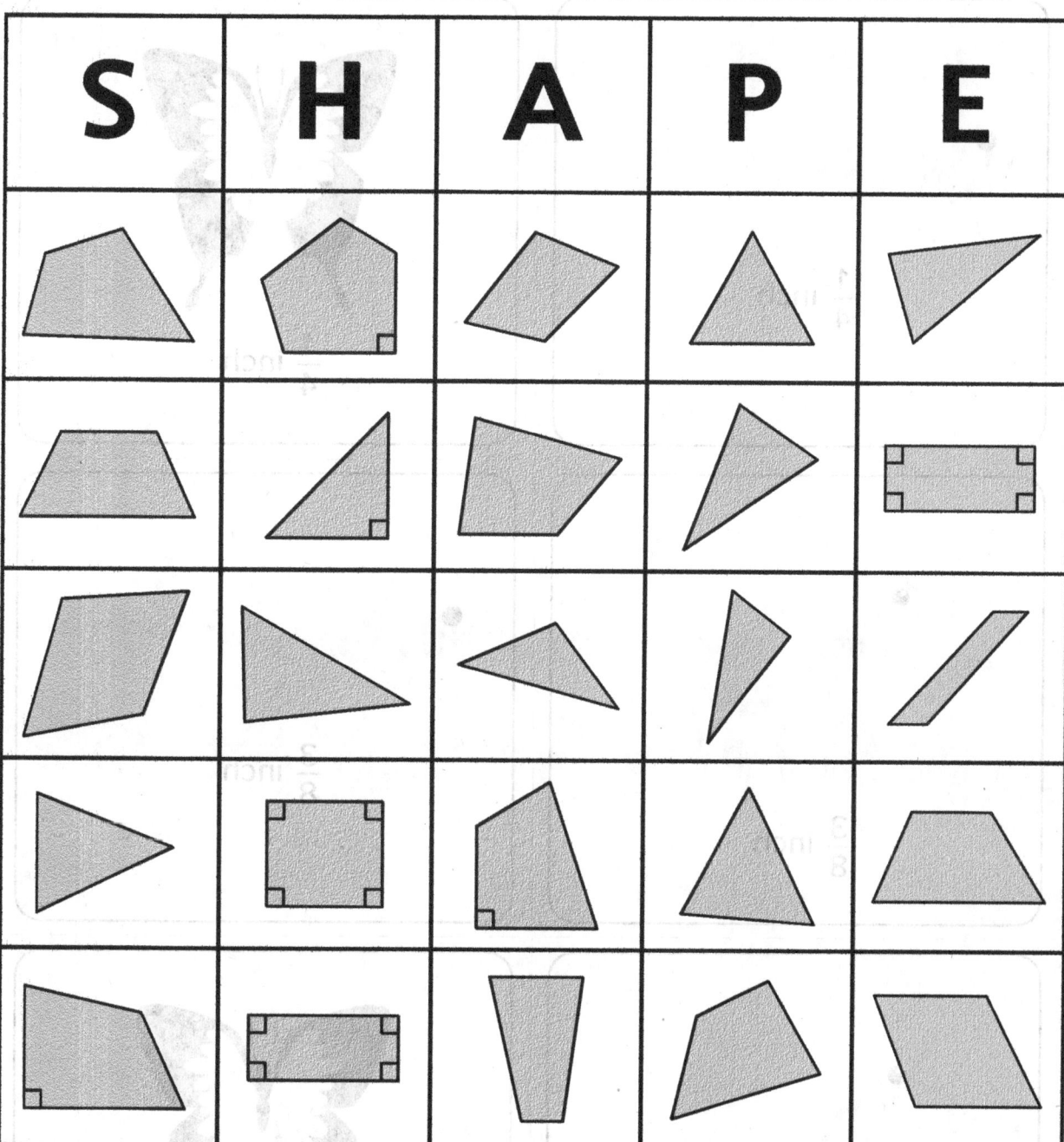

Collection Cards

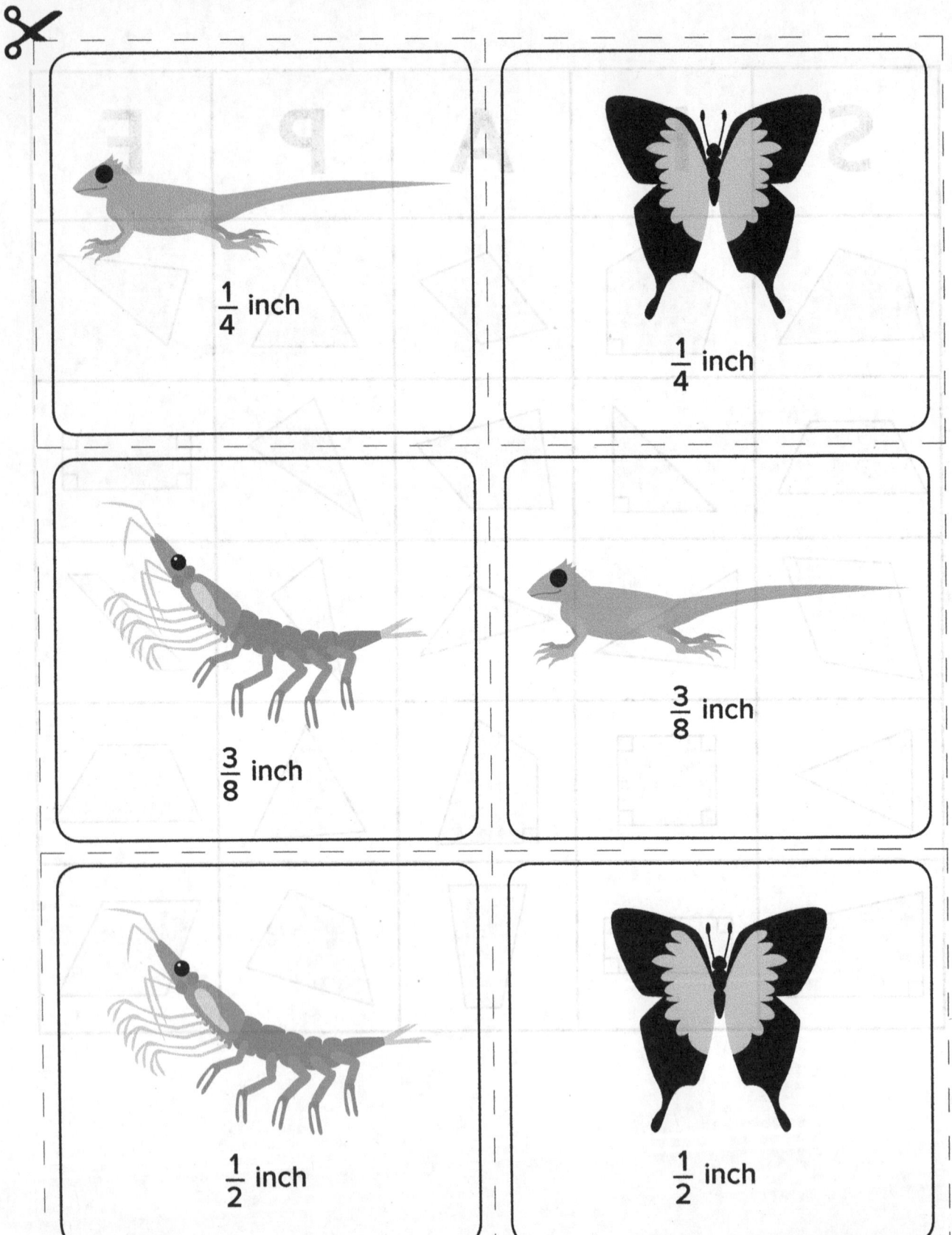

Collection Cards

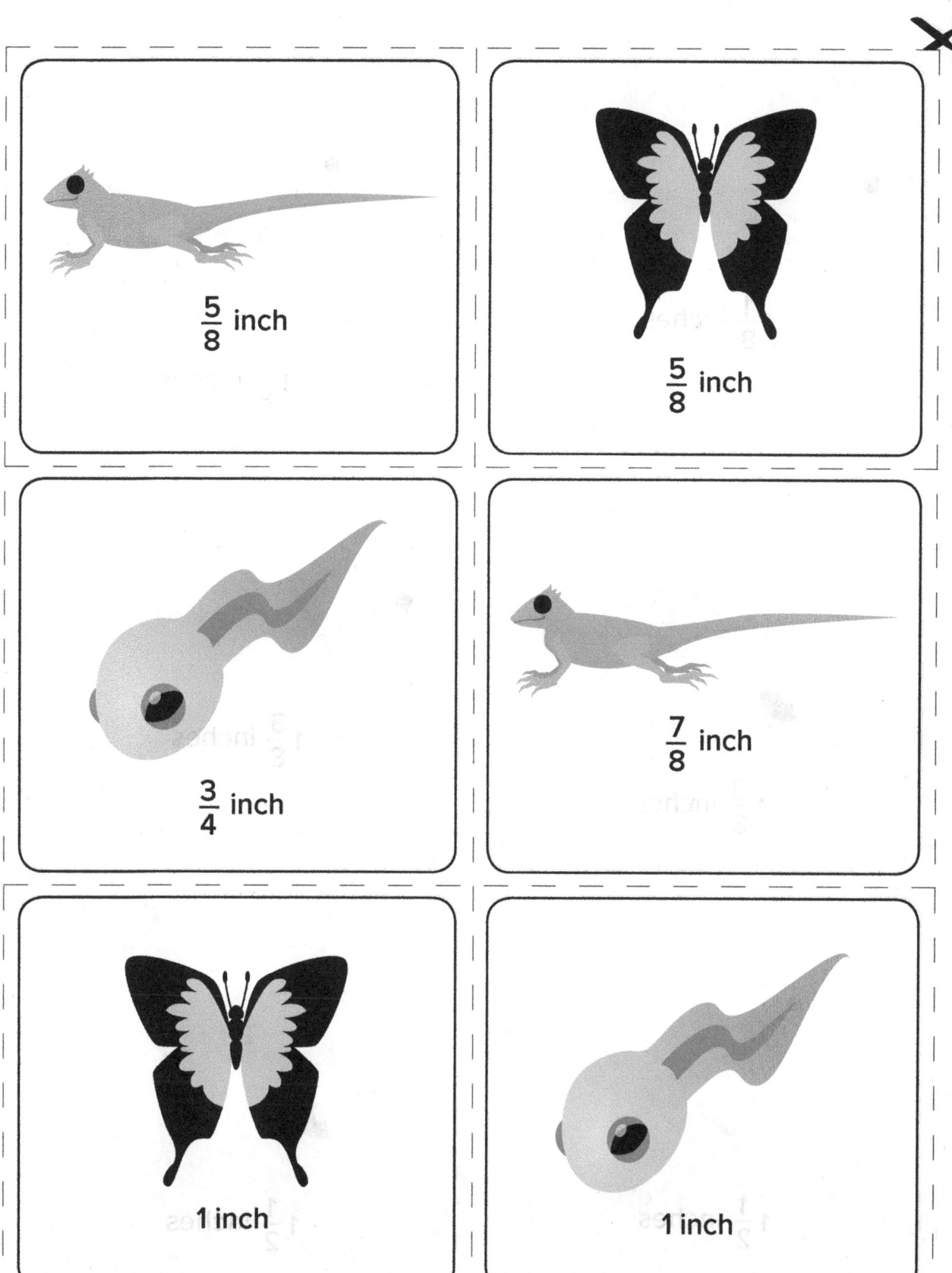

Collection Cards

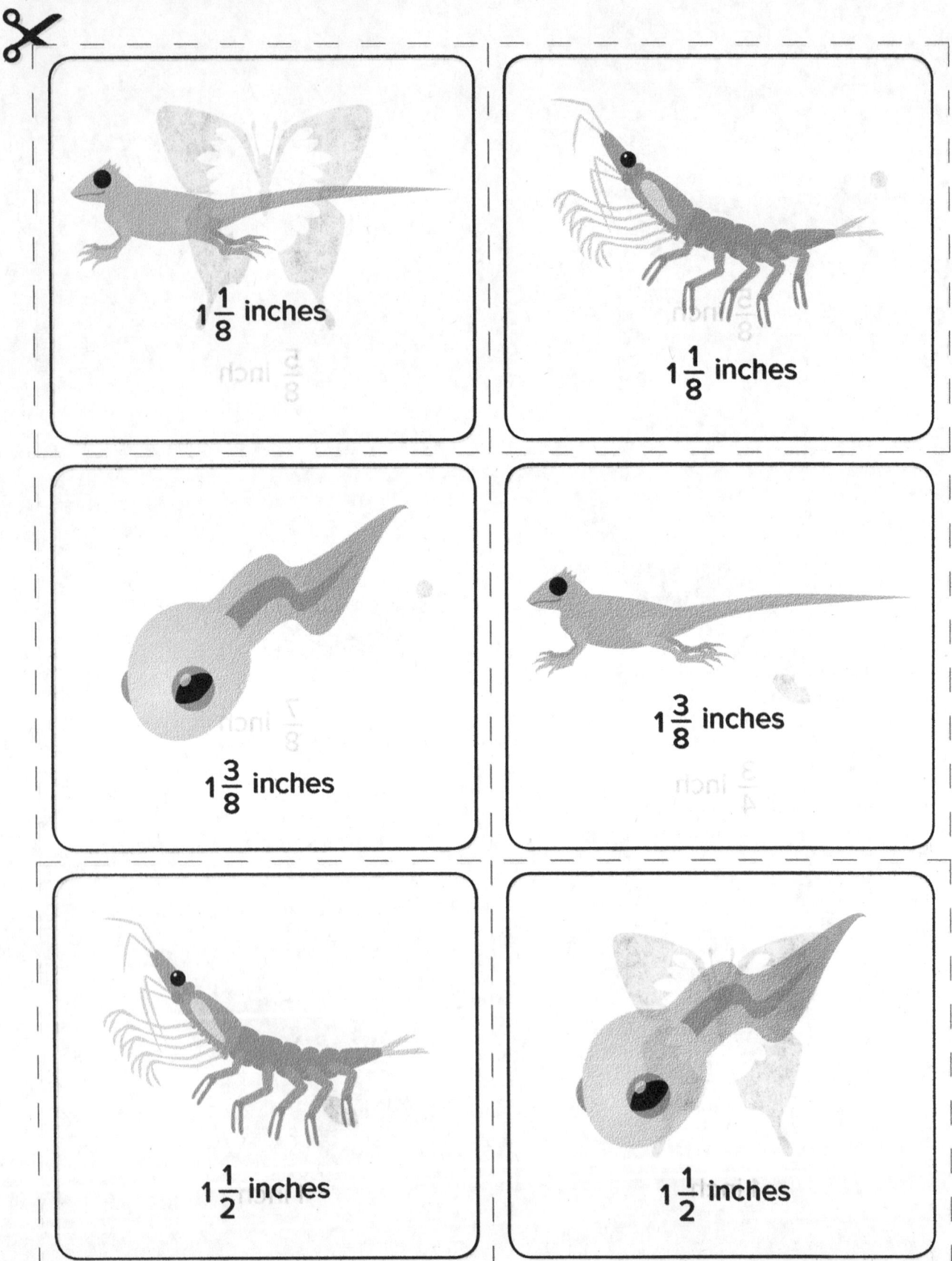

Collection Cards

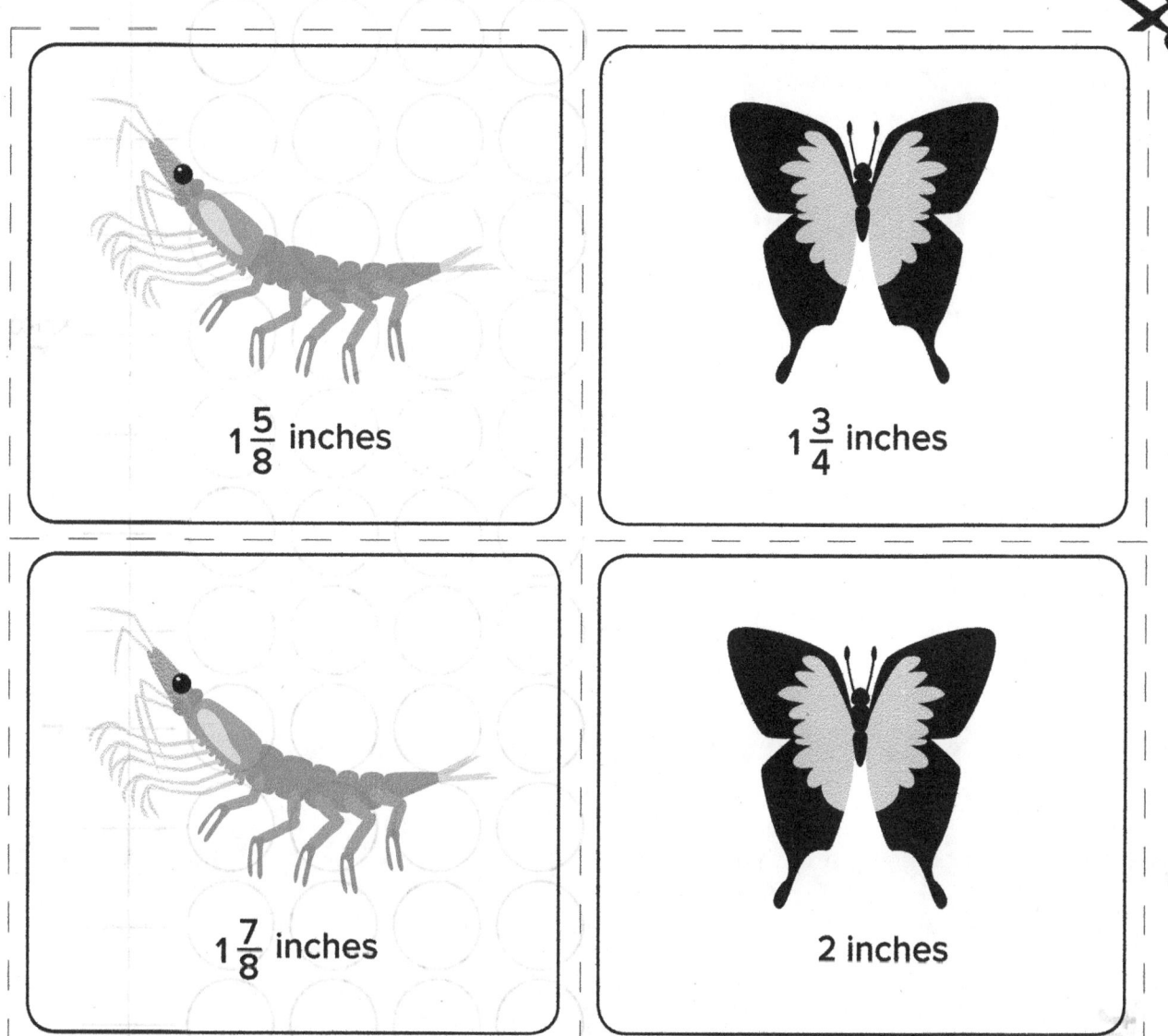

Collection Line Plot

92 Collection Line Plot • **Games Kit Resource Guide**

Decimal Number Cards

7.81	89.83	335.253
6.352	74.128	904.681
5.9	62.8	752.395

Games Kit Resource Guide • Decimal Number Cards (1 of 3)

Decimal Number Cards

8.6	3.42	9.107
49.6	52.7	13.92
157.43	236.52	483.86

Decimal Number Cards

1.7	34.34	521.7
2.54	25.673	617.1
4.993	91.459	868.6

Games Kit Resource Guide • Decimal Number Cards (3 of 3)

Decimal Number Writing Frame

___ × 100 + ___ × 10 + ___ × 1 + (___ × $\frac{1}{10}$) + (___ × $\frac{1}{100}$) = (___ × $\frac{1}{1,000}$)

Sample answer for 356.219 in expanded form:

$\underline{3}$ × 100 + $\underline{5}$ × 10 + $\underline{6}$ × 1 + ($\underline{2}$ × $\frac{1}{10}$) + ($\underline{1}$ × $\frac{1}{100}$) = ($\underline{9}$ × $\frac{1}{1,000}$)

Fraction Mat

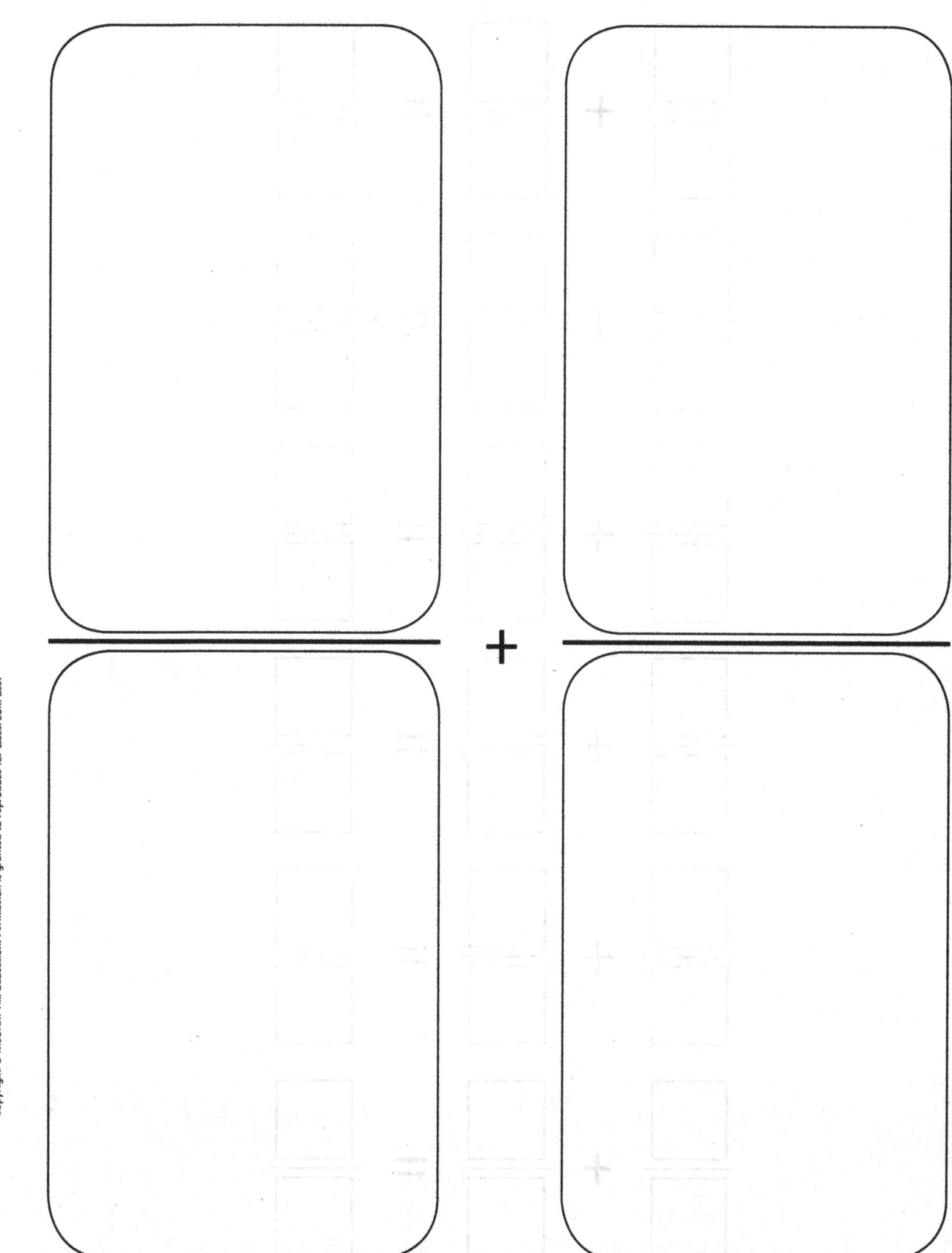

Win Sum Lose Sum Record Sheet

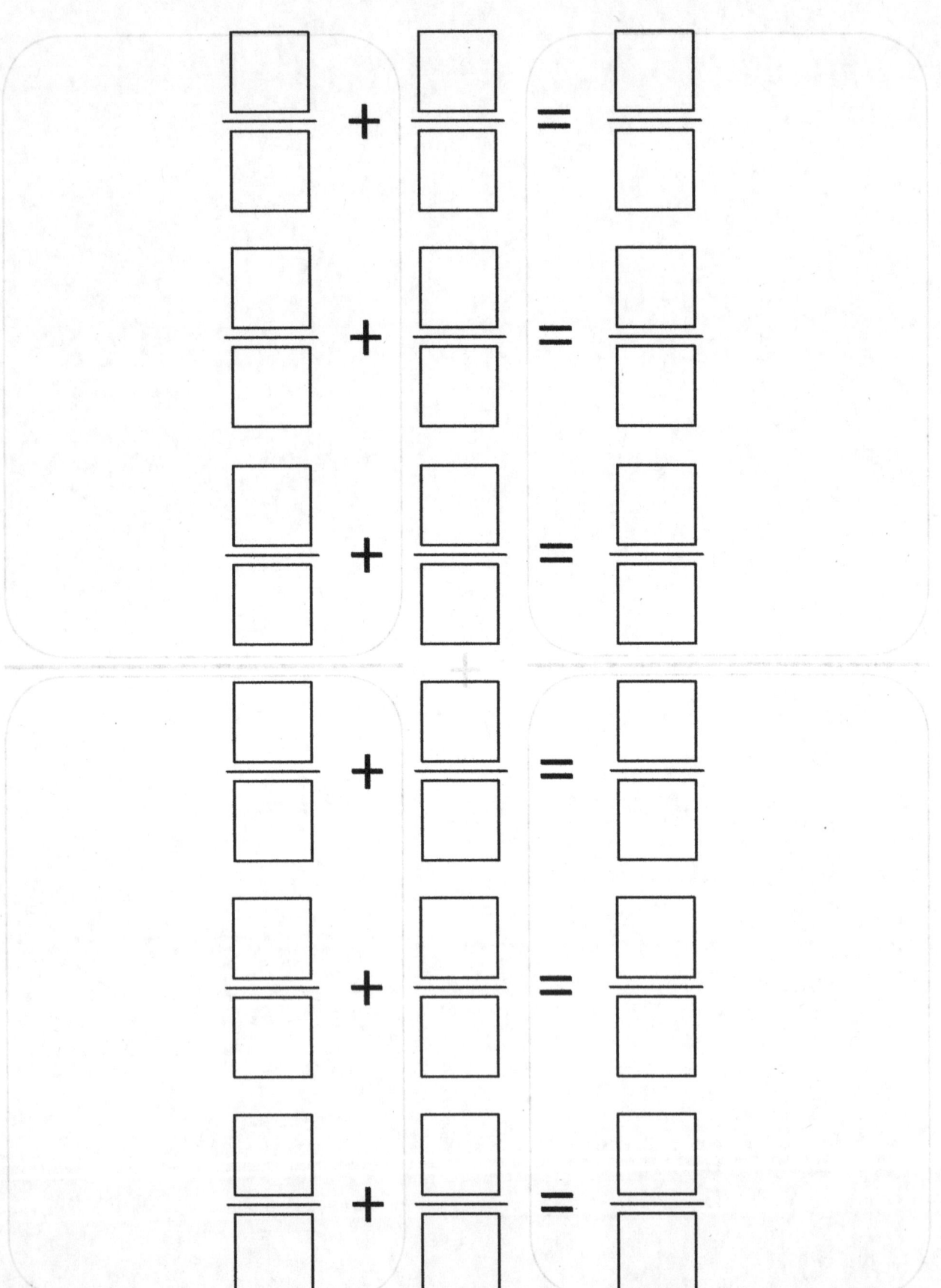

98 Win Sum Lose Sum Record Sheet • **Games Kit Resource Guide**

Basic Expression Record Sheet

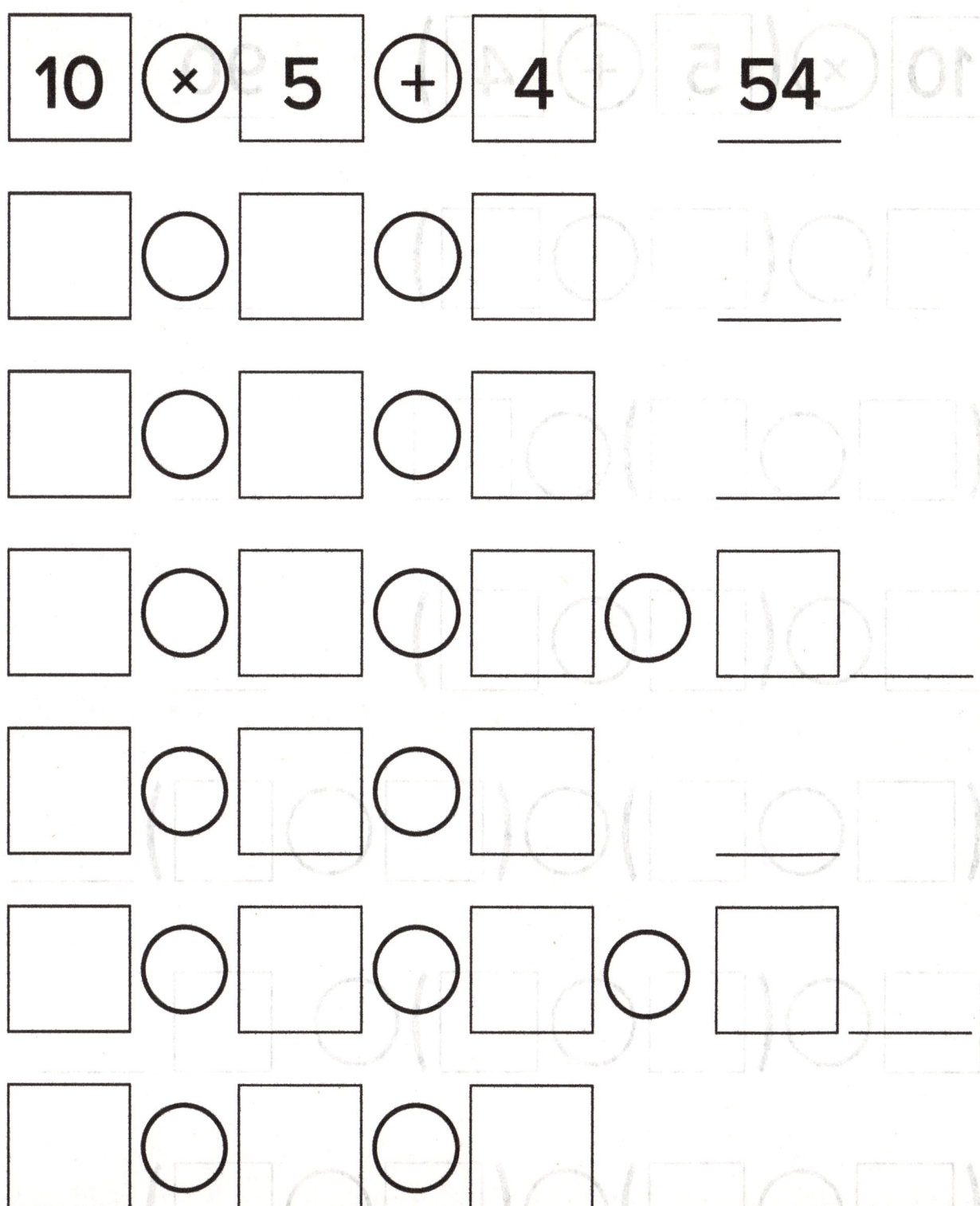

Games Kit Resource Guide • Basic Expression Record Sheet

Expression Record Sheet

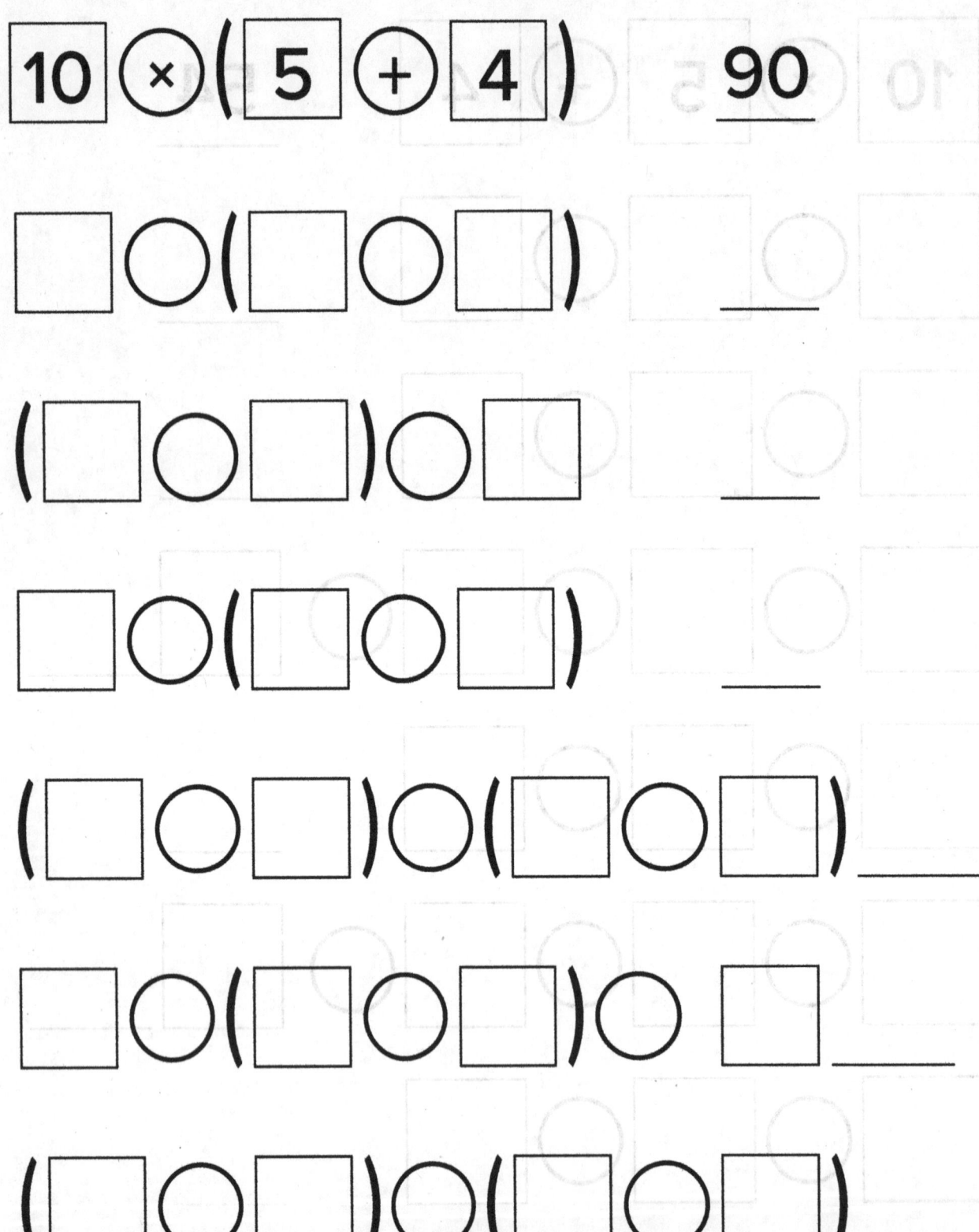

100 Expression Record Sheet • Games Kit Resource Guide

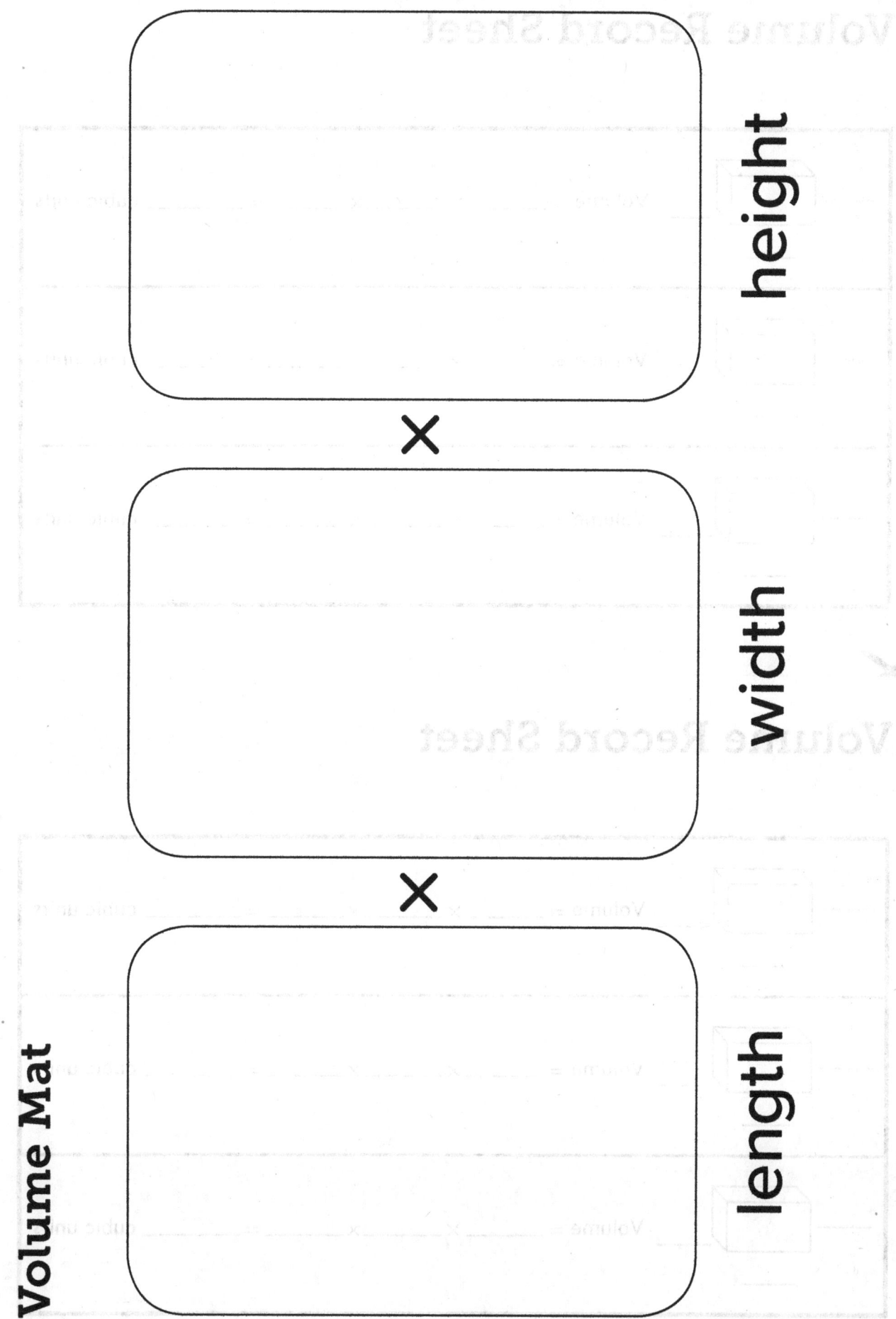

Games Kit Resource Guide • Volume Mat

Volume Record Sheet

____ Volume = ____ × ____ × ____ = ____ cubic units

____ Volume = ____ × ____ × ____ = ____ cubic units

____ Volume = ____ × ____ × ____ = ____ cubic units

✂ -

Volume Record Sheet

____ Volume = ____ × ____ × ____ = ____ cubic units

____ Volume = ____ × ____ × ____ = ____ cubic units

____ Volume = ____ × ____ × ____ = ____ cubic units

102 Volume Record Sheet • **Games Kit Resource Guide**

Fraction Sums and Differences

$\frac{2}{8} + \frac{3}{8}$	$\frac{7}{8} + \frac{1}{8}$	$\frac{3}{8} + \frac{4}{8}$	$\frac{5}{8} + \frac{2}{8}$	$\frac{2}{8} + \frac{3}{8}$
$\frac{2}{8} + \frac{1}{8}$	$\frac{1}{8} + \frac{1}{8}$	$\frac{3}{4} + \frac{1}{8}$	$\frac{2}{4} + \frac{2}{8}$	$\frac{1}{4} + \frac{2}{8}$
$\frac{1}{4} + \frac{1}{8}$	$\frac{4}{8} + \frac{1}{2}$	$\frac{1}{2} + \frac{3}{8}$	$\frac{1}{2} + \frac{2}{8}$	$\frac{1}{2} + \frac{1}{8}$
$\frac{1}{2} + \frac{1}{4}$	$\frac{3}{4} + \frac{1}{4}$	$\frac{1}{4} + \frac{2}{4}$	$\frac{1}{4} + \frac{1}{4}$	$\frac{1}{2} + \frac{1}{2}$

Fraction Sums and Differences

$\dfrac{6}{8} + \dfrac{5}{8}$	$\dfrac{5}{8} + \dfrac{4}{8}$	$\dfrac{7}{8} - \dfrac{2}{8}$	$\dfrac{6}{8} - \dfrac{1}{8}$	$\dfrac{4}{8} + \dfrac{2}{8}$
$\dfrac{7}{8} - \dfrac{6}{8}$	$\dfrac{4}{8} - \dfrac{1}{8}$	$\dfrac{5}{8} - \dfrac{2}{8}$	$\dfrac{7}{8} - \dfrac{1}{8}$	$\dfrac{8}{8} - \dfrac{1}{8}$
$\dfrac{4}{8} + \dfrac{1}{2}$	$\dfrac{6}{8} + \dfrac{1}{2}$	$\dfrac{5}{8} + \dfrac{1}{2}$	$\dfrac{1}{2} + \dfrac{3}{8}$	$\dfrac{1}{2} - \dfrac{1}{8}$
$\dfrac{7}{8} - \dfrac{3}{4}$	$\dfrac{2}{4} + \dfrac{3}{8}$	$\dfrac{3}{4} - \dfrac{2}{8}$	$\dfrac{1}{2} - \dfrac{1}{4}$	$\dfrac{1}{4} + \dfrac{1}{8}$

Solution Record Sheet

Expression	Sum or Difference	Used
		☐
		☐
		☐
		☐
		☐
		☐
		☐
		☐
		☐
		☐
		☐
		☐

Climbing Capture Problem Cards

The football team lost x yard(s). The change to their position is _____ yard(s).

Sam's house was built x meter(s) above sea level. The elevation is _____ meter(s).

The temperature is x° below 0. The temperature is _____ °F.

Pia took x pictures on her phone. The change in the amount of pictures on her phone is represented by _____.

The family cabin is x yard(s) below sea level. The elevation is _____ yard(s).

Lilly deleted x pictures on her phone. The change in the amount of pictures on her phone is represented by _____.

The opposite of x is _____.

Mateo earned $x for delivering newspapers. Mateo's bank account changed by $_____.

The opposite of −x is _____.

Climbing Capture Problem Cards

Margaret moved back x space(s) on a game board. This move can be represented by _____.

The parking garage is x floor(s) high. The height of the building is _____ floor(s).

The opposite of x is _____.

The number x more than 0 is _____.

The opposite of −x is _____.

The opposite of x is _____.

−x is _____ away from 0.

---

x is _____ away from 0.

Jeremy's hot air balloon moved down x yard(s). This move can be representd by _____.

Climbing Capture Problem Cards

The number x less than 0 is ____.

The opposite of x is ____.

Cari's team gained x yard(s) on the play. The team's position changed by ____ yard(s).

Bella built a sandcastle that was x feet high. The height of the sandcastle was ____ feet.

The value of −(x) is ____.

The temperature increased by x degree(s). The temperature changed by ____ degree(s).

−x is ____ away from 0.

Jake's team won x games this month. The amount of wins changed by ____ this month.

Climbing Capture Problem Cards

The dive team dove x meter(s) below sea level. Their elevation is _____ meter(s).

The temperature decreased by x degree(s). The temperature change can be represented by _____ degree(s).

Katie earned $\$x$ from selling magazines. Katie's bank account changed by $\$ _____.

Li's team lost x games this month. The change in the team's record can be represented by _____.

The value of $-(x)$ is _____.

Mack lost x points while playing a video game. The change in his score can be represented by _____.

The number x more than 0 is _____.

The number x less than 0 is _____.

The opposite of $-x$ is _____.

Ratio Bingo Cards

Carrie's green paint is 2 parts blue to 1 part yellow. What is the ratio of blue to yellow paint?

Pineapples cost $6 for 2. What ratio shows the unit price for a pineapple?

The hockey team has 6 male players and 10 female players. What is the ratio of male to female players?

Mark's soup recipe uses 3 potatoes for every 2 carrots. What is the ratio of potatoes to carrots in the soup?

The hair salon uses 2 bottles of shampoo and 5 bottles of conditioner every week. What is the ratio of shampoo used to conditioner used?

The bulk store charges $8 for 2 bags of rice. What ratio shows the unit price for a bag of rice?

Imani's tea recipe uses 8 tea bags for every 10 cups of water. What is the ratio of tea bags to cups of water?

The basketball team has an equal number of left- and right-handed players. What is the ratio of left-handed players to right-handed players?

Ratio Bingo Cards

1 : 4

3 : 4

2 : 3

9 : 3

A diner sells 3 salads for every 4 sandwiches it sells. What is the ratio of salad to sandwich sales?

A bag contains 4 red balls for every 6 green balls. What is the ratio of red to green balls?

The soup recipe uses 5 cups of vegetables and 10 cups of stock. What is the ratio of vegetables to stock?

A class has 3 math books for every 5 English books. What is the ratio of math books to English books?

Ratio Bingo Cards

1 : 2	4 : 10
1 : 3	3 : 1
4 : 6	3 : 2
2 : 4	4 : 2

Ratio Bingo Cards

The track team practices 3 days then takes 2 days off. What is the ratio of practice days to days off?

A student answered 6 questions correctly for every 4 questions he answered incorrectly. What is the ratio of correct to incorrect answers?

The sauce had 2 tablespoon of butter and 4 tablespoons of milk. What is the ratio of butter to milk?

The purple paint uses 2 parts red to 8 parts blue. What is the ratio of red to blue paint?

The debate team has 3 fifth-grade and 3 seventh-grade students. What is the ratio of fifth graders to seventh graders?

The pizza shop uses 2 slices of salami for every 6 slices of pepperoni on a pizza. What is the ratio of salami to pepperoni?

The volleyball team has 8 away games and 10 home games. What is the ratio of away games to home games?

A carpenter uses 4 feet of maple lumber and 5 feet of pine lumber to make a table. What is the ratio of maple to pine lumber?

Ratio Bingo Cards

2 : 2	3 : 3
6 : 10	3 : 5
6 : 4	1 : 4
6 : 8	3 : 6

Ratio Bingo Mat

2:5	4:5	6:2	6:10	4:6
3:1	1:2	2:8	6:3	3:2
1:3	4:2	Free	6:8	8:4
4:4	3:4	3:6	2:3	2:4
8:12	6:4	9:3	8:10	3:5

Ratio Bingo Mat

3:5	2:3	9:3	6:2	8:12
6:4	6:8	2:5	3:5	3:1
6:2	1:3	Free	2:8	6:10
3:4	4:2	4:4	3:2	1:2
2:4	8:8	4:5	4:6	6:3

Ratio Bingo Mat

6:2	6:10	4:1	1:2	2:3
6:3	2:8	3:4	1:3	2:5
3:5	8:4	Free	2:5	6:4
4:4	3:6	4:6	3:1	2:4
4:5	3:2	8:10	4:2	3:5

Ratio Bingo Mat

9:3	3:4	3:5	4:10
4:5	2:5	3:6	3:4
6:3	3:1	Free	4:1
1:3	6:8	2:8	8:12	8:4
2:3	6:4	6:2	2:5	1:2

Area Trek Cards

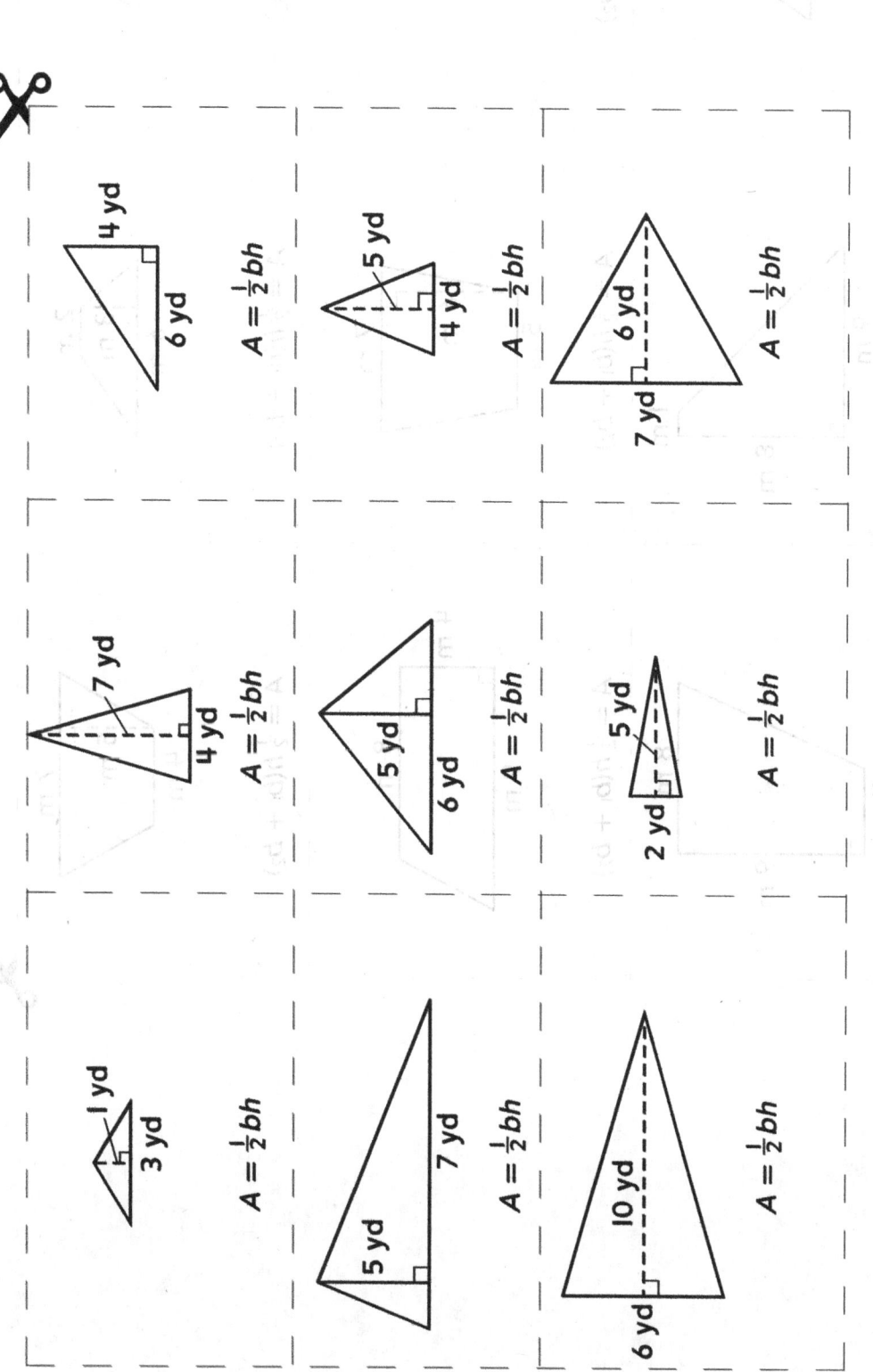

Games Kit Resource Guide • Area Trek Cards (1 of 4)

Area Trek Cards

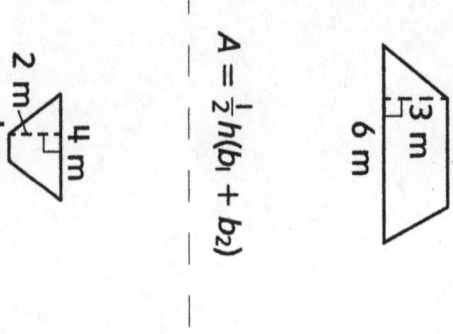

$A = \frac{1}{2}h(b_1 + b_2)$

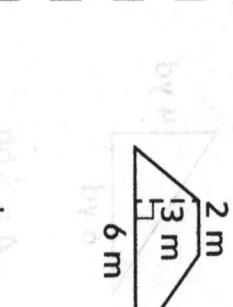

$A = \frac{1}{2}h(b_1 + b_2)$

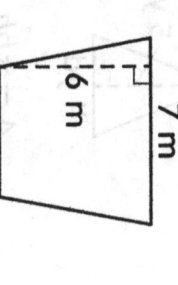

$A = \frac{1}{2}h(b_1 + b_2)$

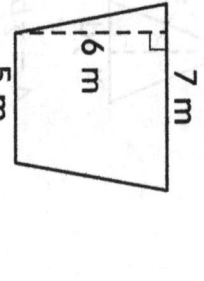

$A = \frac{1}{2}h(b_1 + b_2)$

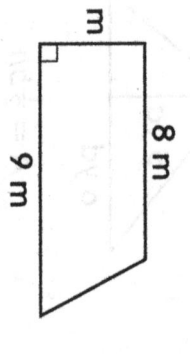

$A = \frac{1}{2}h(b_1 + b_2)$

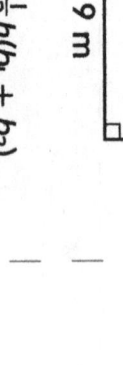

$A = \frac{1}{2}h(b_1 + b_2)$

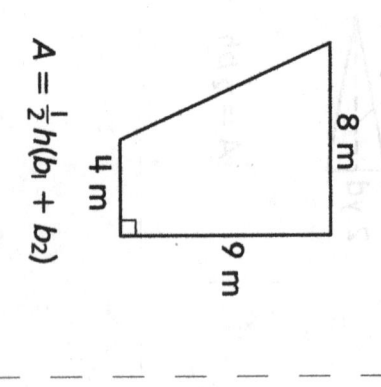

$A = \frac{1}{2}h(b_1 + b_2)$

Area Trek Cards

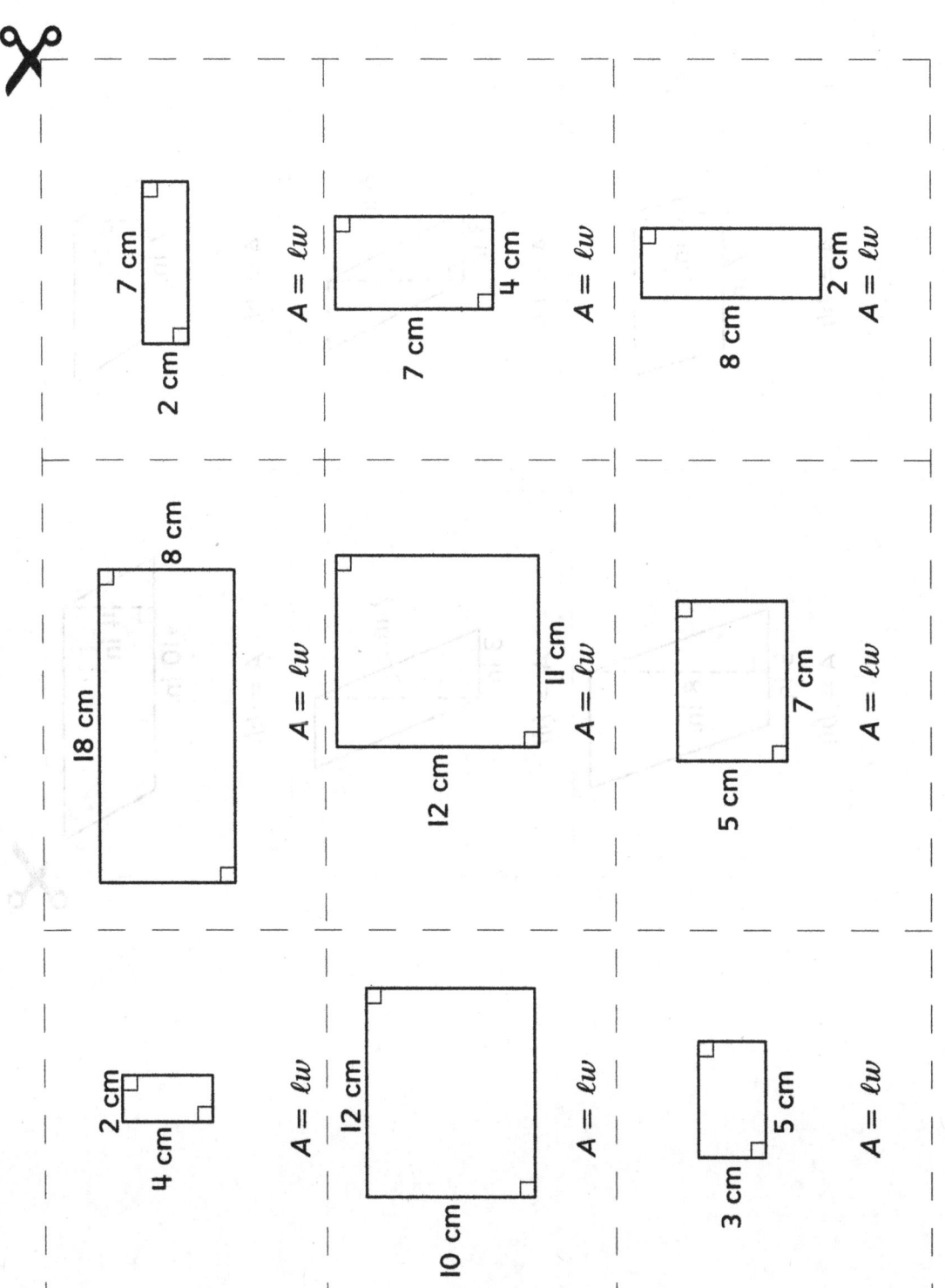

Area Trek Cards

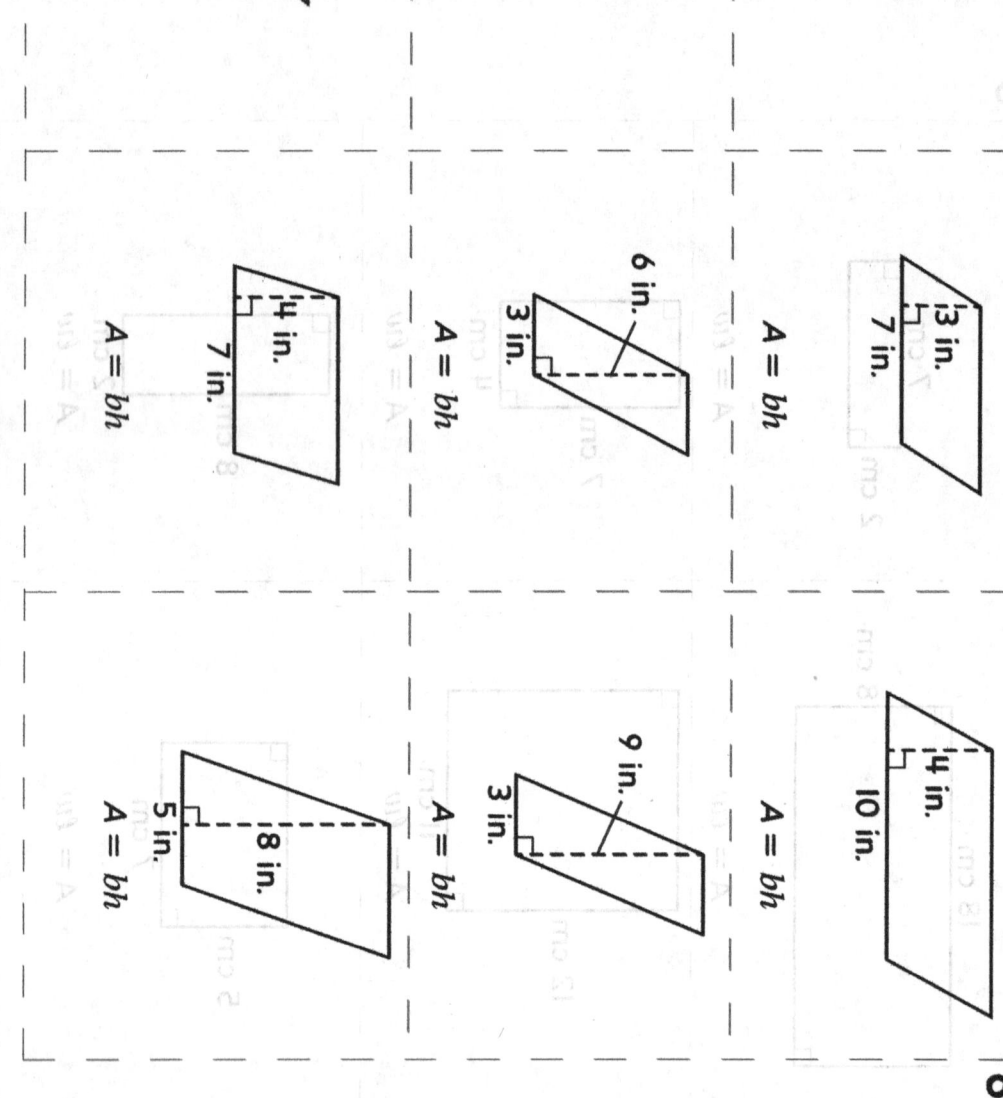

Surface Area Cards

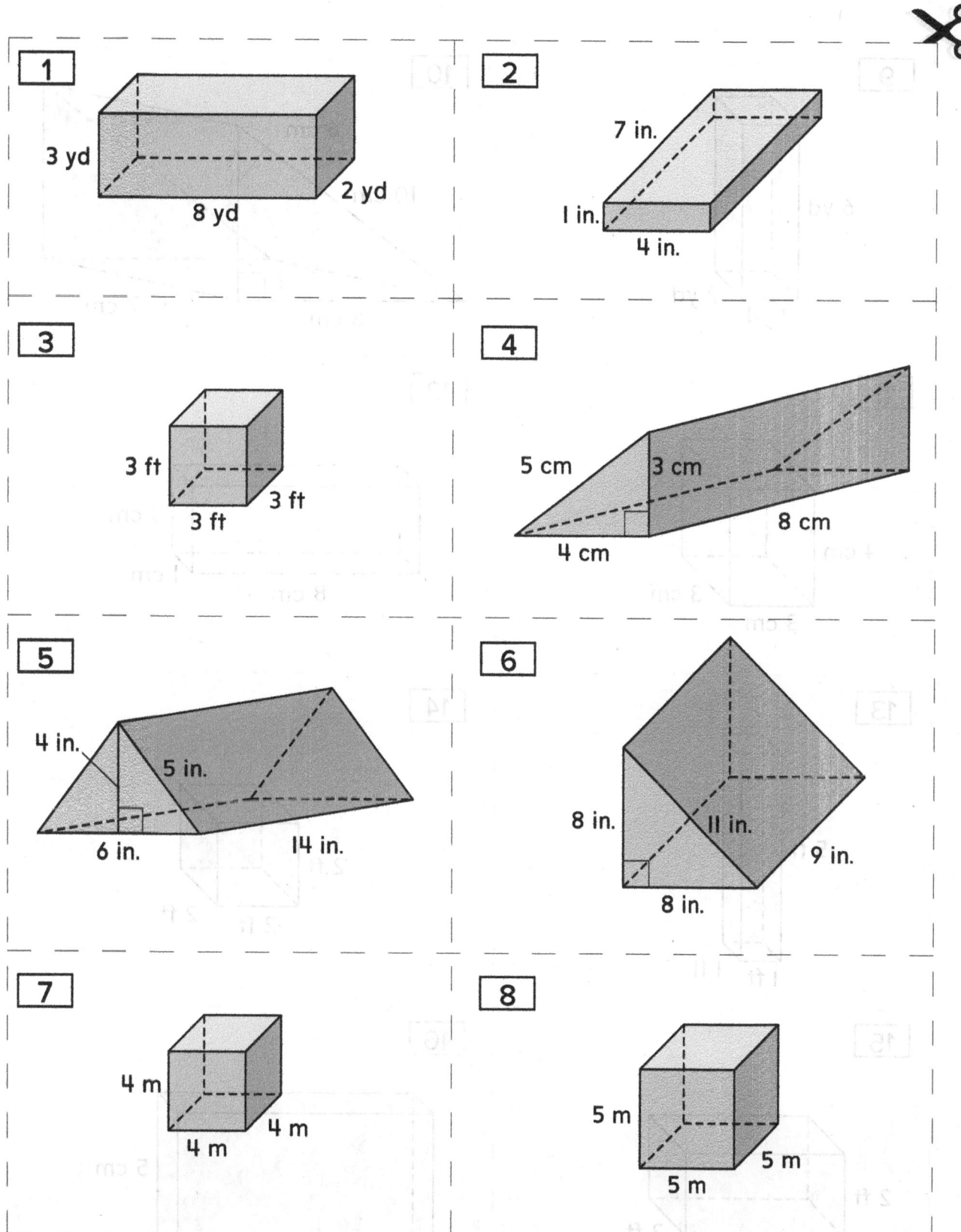

Surface Area Cards

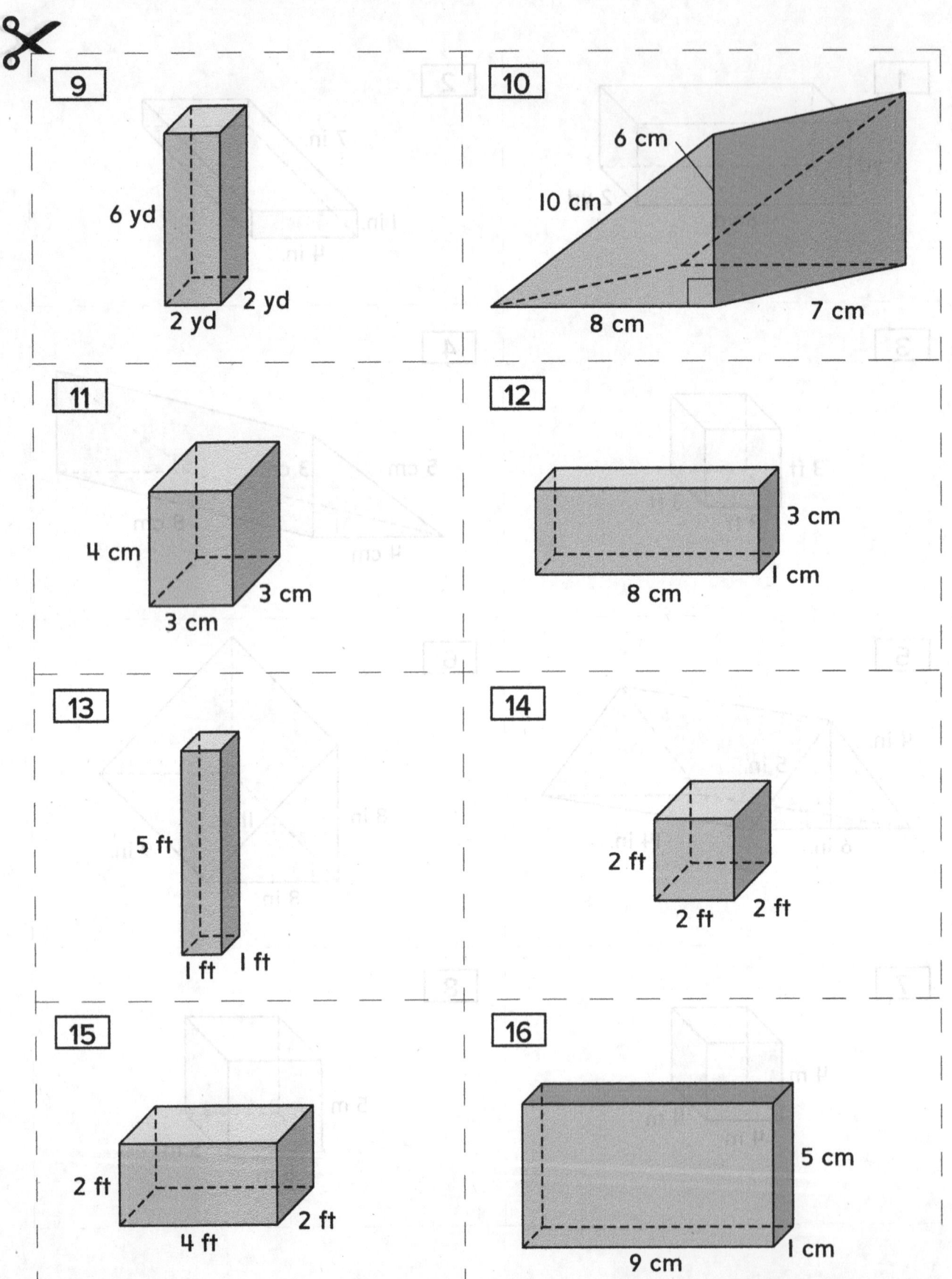

Surface Area Cards

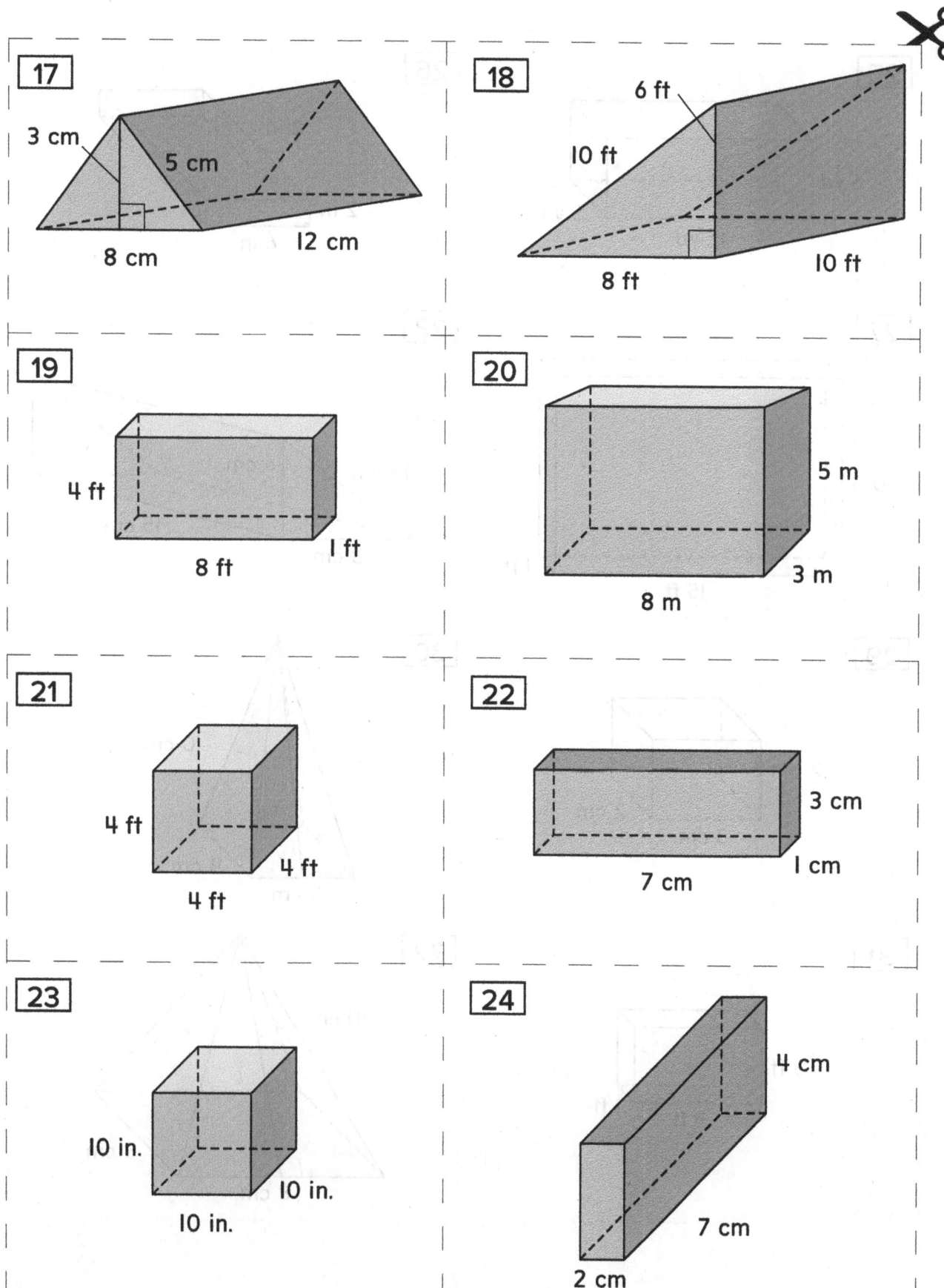

Surface Area Cards

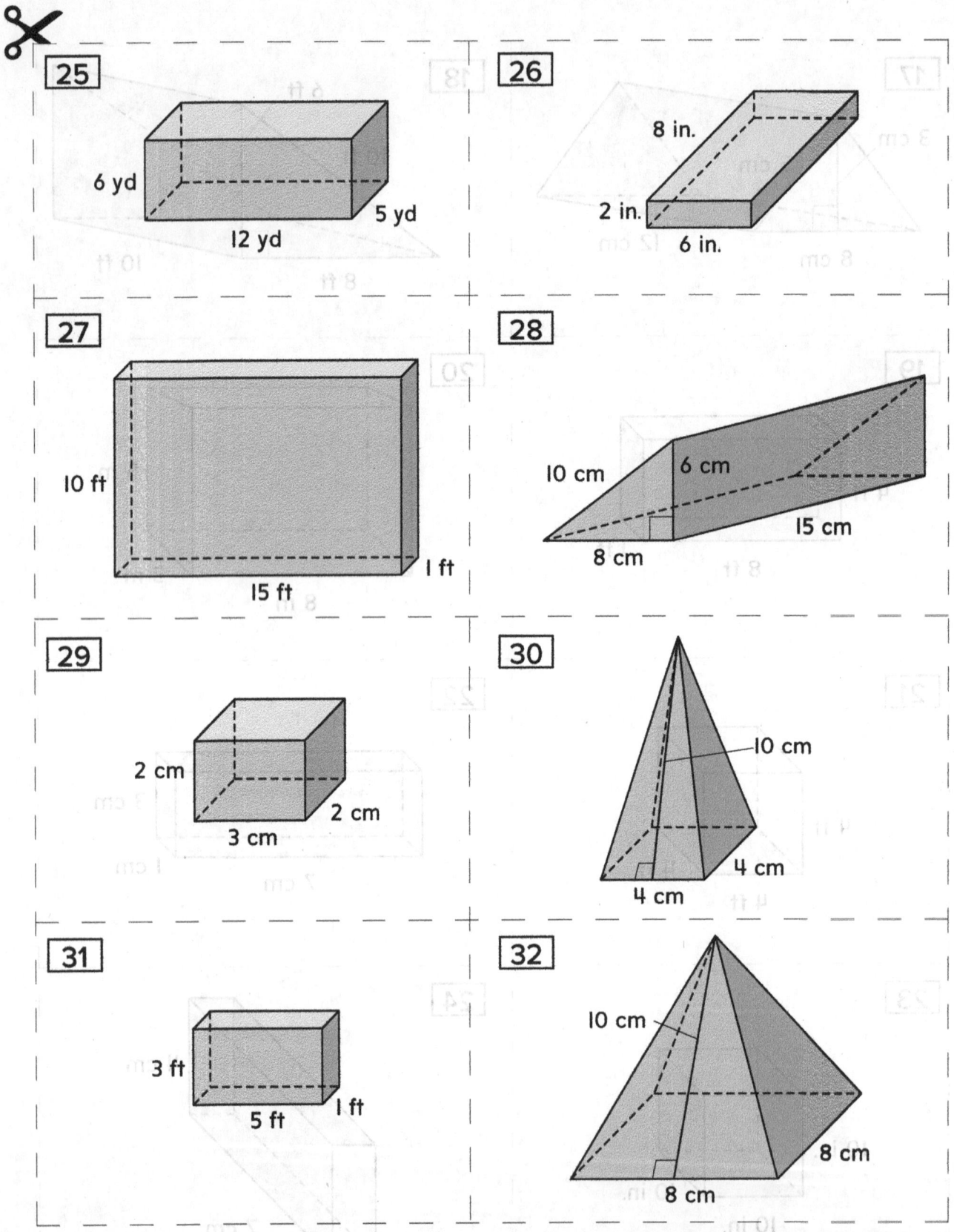

Surface Area Cards

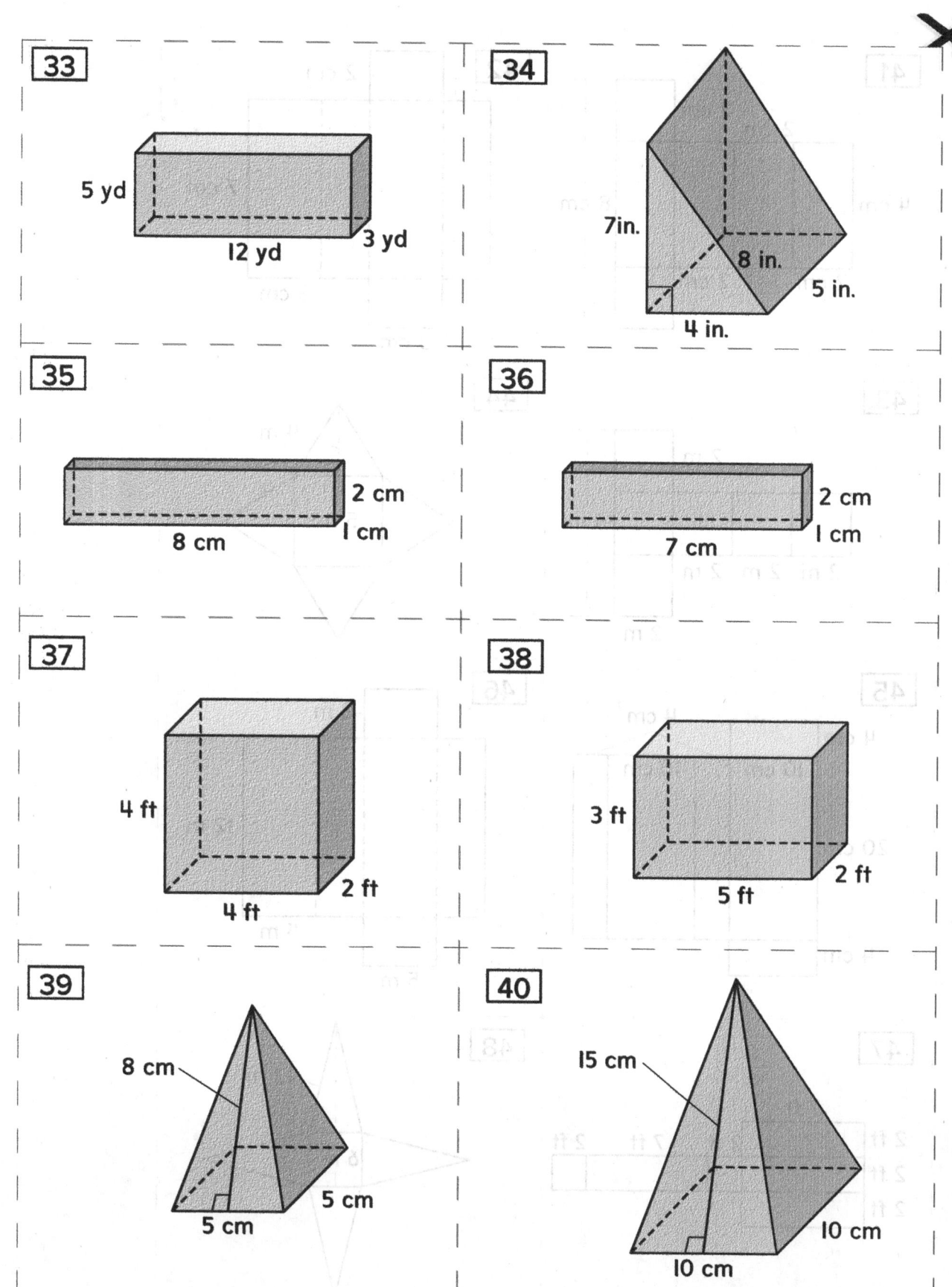

Surface Area Cards

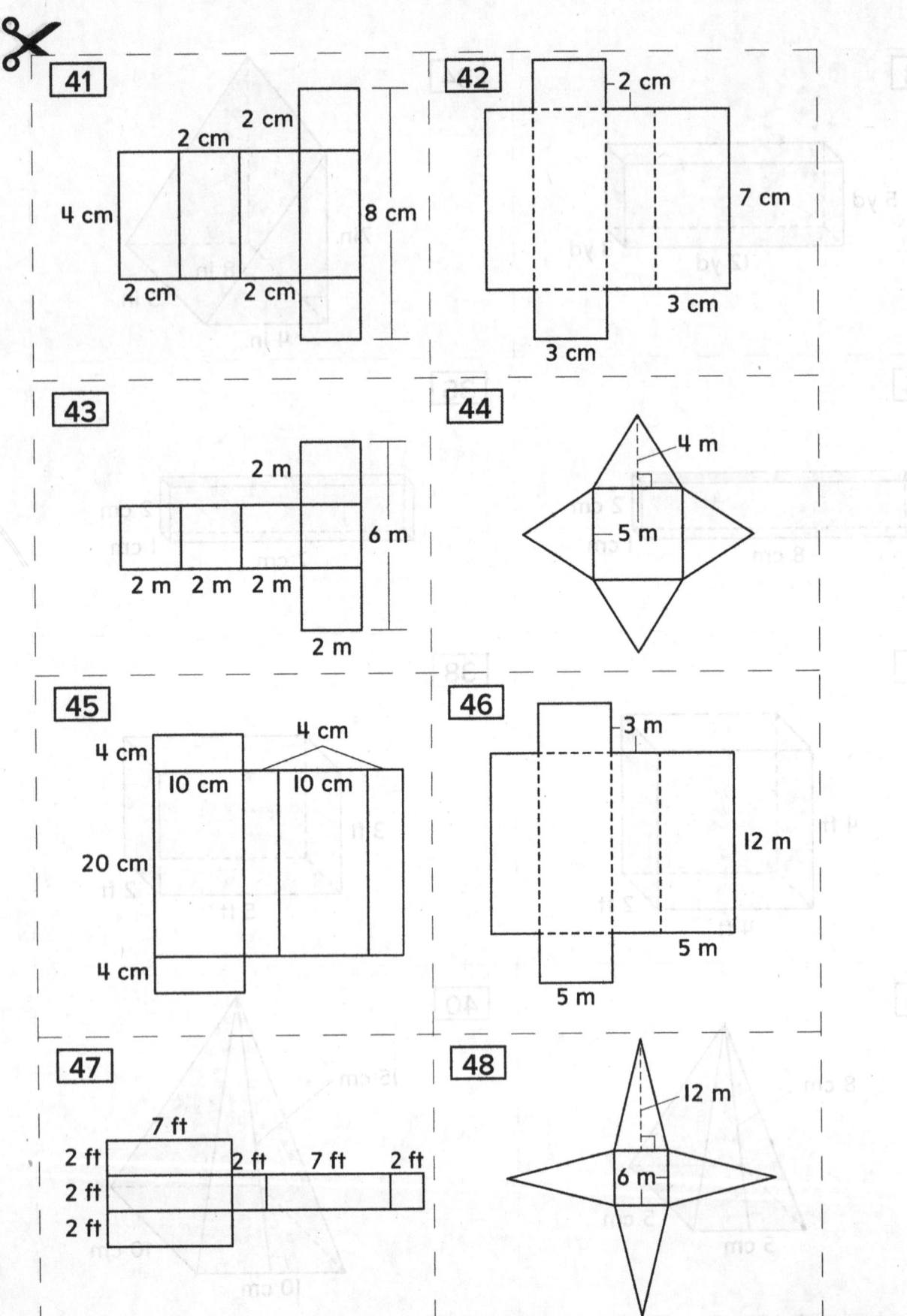

Surface Area Cards Answer Key

1. 92 yd²
2. 78 in²
3. 54 ft²
4. 108 cm²
5. 248 in²
6. 307 in²
7. 96 m²
8. 150 m²
9. 56 yd²
10. 216 cm²
11. 66 cm²
12. 70 cm²
13. 22 ft²
14. 24 ft²
15. 40 ft²
16. 118 cm²
17. 240 cm²
18. 288 ft²
19. 88 ft²
20. 158 m²
21. 96 ft²
22. 62 cm²
23. 600 in²
24. 100 cm²
25. 324 yd²
26. 152 in²
27. 350 ft²
28. 408 cm²
29. 32 cm²
30. 96 cm²
31. 46 ft²
32. 224 cm²
33. 222 yd²
34. 123 in²
35. 52 cm²
36. 46 cm²
37. 64 ft²
38. 62 ft²
39. 105 cm²
40. 400 cm²
41. 40 cm²
42. 82 cm²
43. 24 m²
44. 65 m²
45. 640 cm²
46. 222 m²
47. 64 ft²
48. 180 m²

Absolutely Rational Record Sheet

Expression	Solution
____ ▢ ____	
____ ▢ ____	
____ ▢ ____	
____ ▢ ____	
____ ▢ ____	

_____ + _____ + _____ = _____

Rational Number Cards

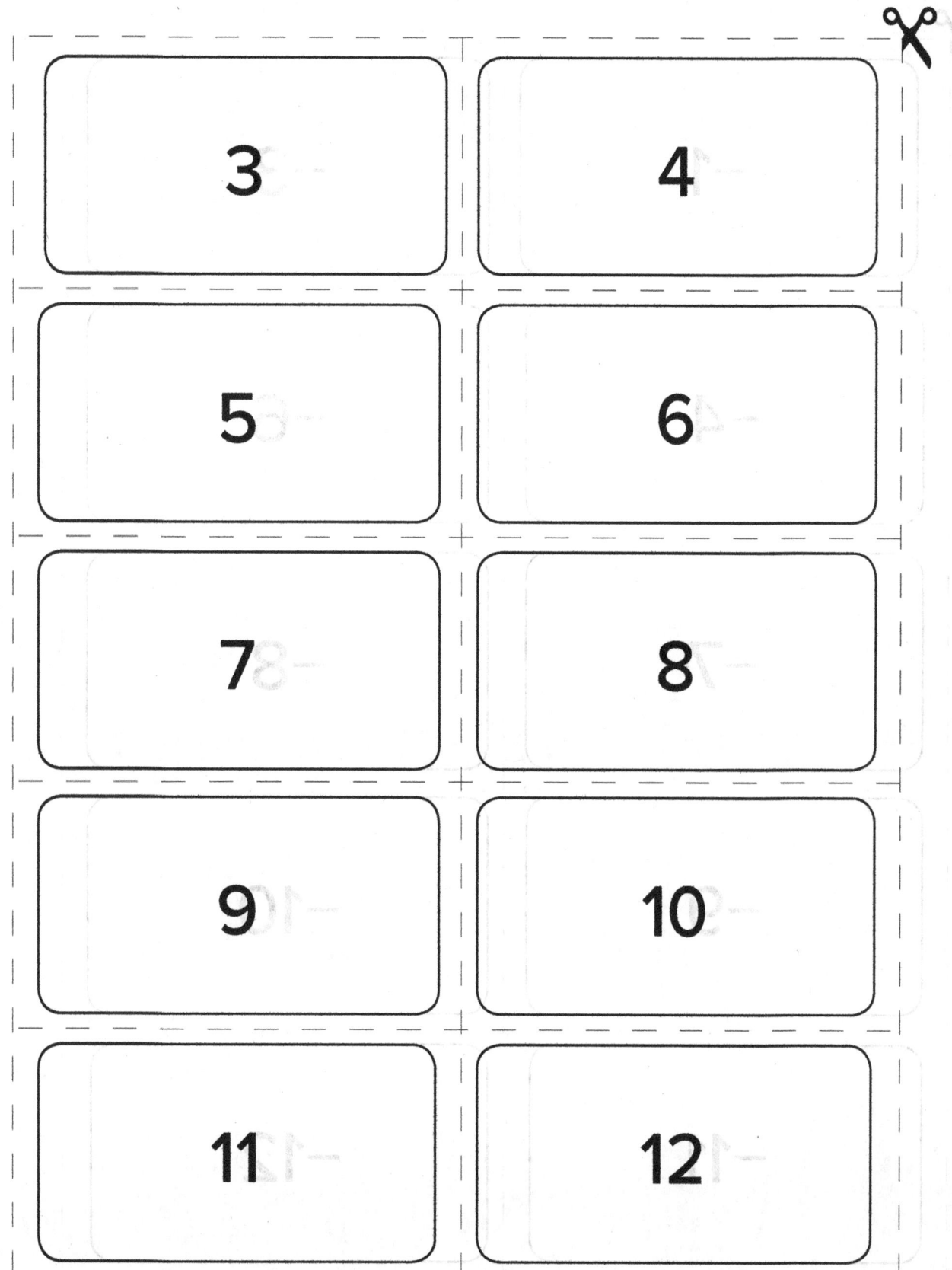

Rational Number Cards

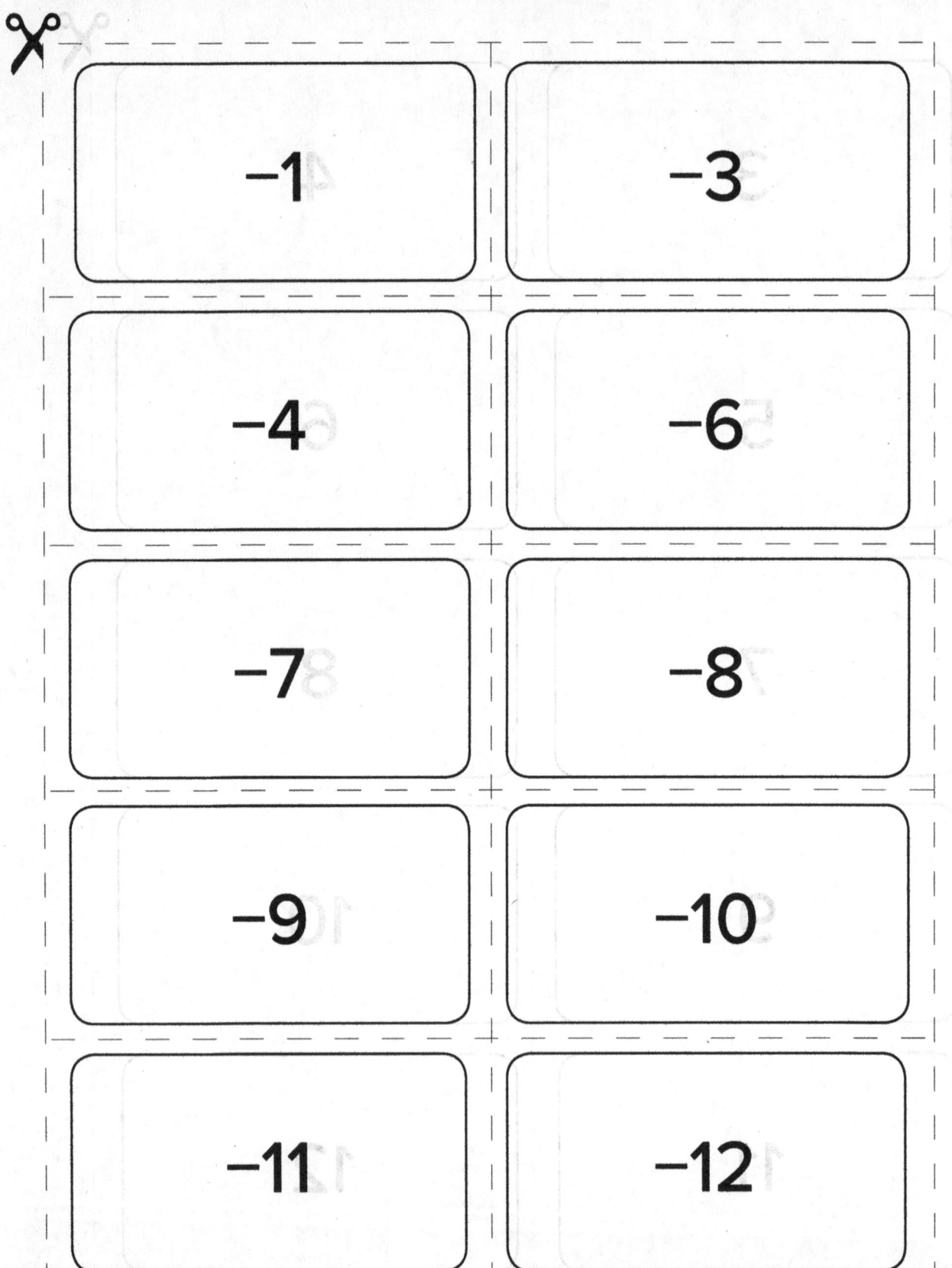

Rational Number Cards

1.5	2.1
3.4	4.5
5.5	6.2
7.8	8.1
9.3	9.7

Rational Number Cards

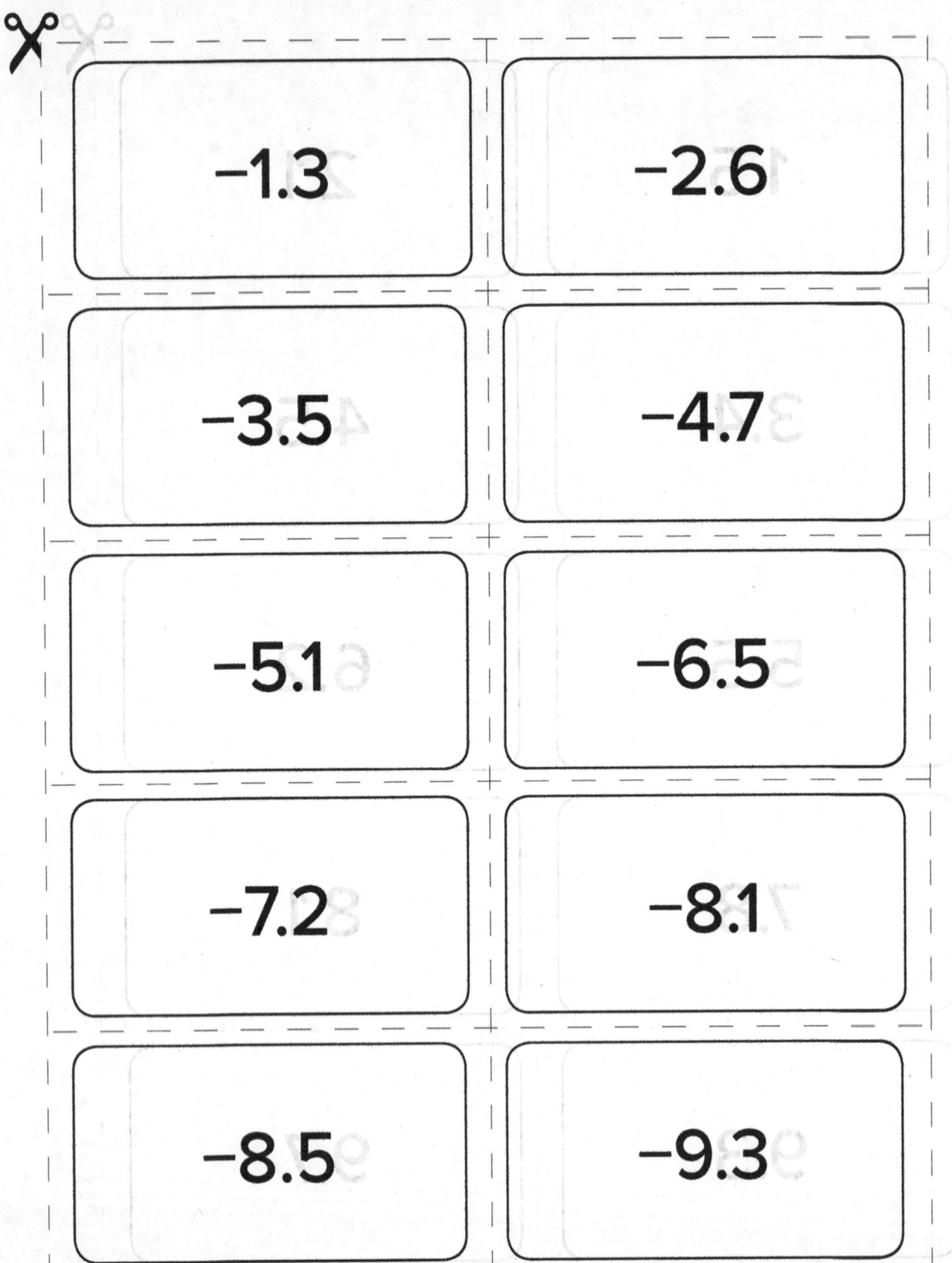

Rational Number Cards

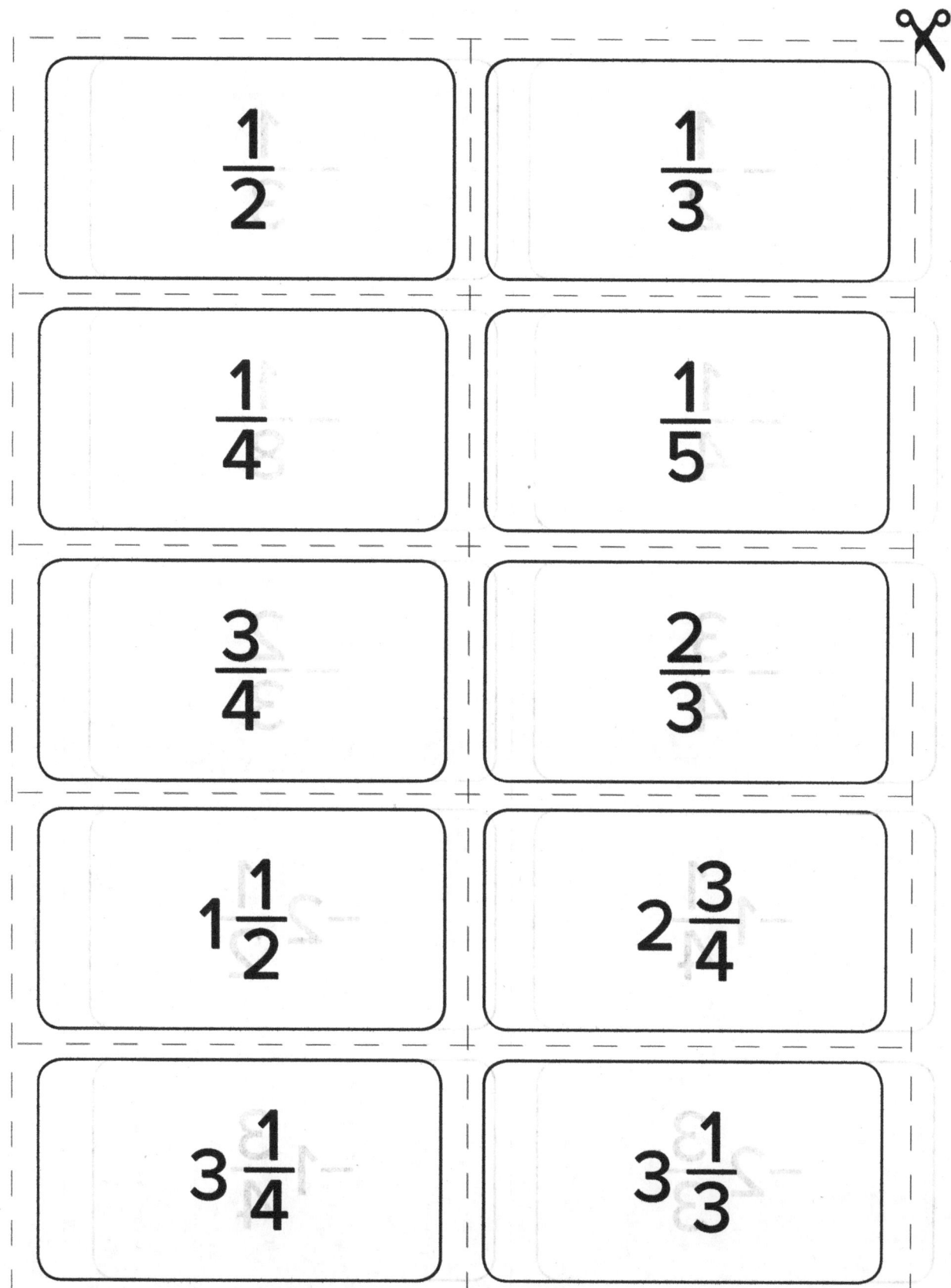

$\frac{1}{2}$	$\frac{1}{3}$
$\frac{1}{4}$	$\frac{1}{5}$
$\frac{3}{4}$	$\frac{2}{3}$
$1\frac{1}{2}$	$2\frac{3}{4}$
$3\frac{1}{4}$	$3\frac{1}{3}$

Rational Number Cards

$-\dfrac{1}{2}$	$-\dfrac{1}{3}$
$-\dfrac{1}{4}$	$-\dfrac{1}{8}$
$-\dfrac{3}{4}$	$-\dfrac{2}{3}$
$-1\dfrac{1}{4}$	$-2\dfrac{1}{2}$
$-2\dfrac{3}{3}$	$-1\dfrac{3}{4}$

Expression Expert Cards

Expression A	Expression A
$54.3 - a$	$15 + g$
Expression B	Expression B
$5 - 9 + a$	$3 + d - 2$
Expression C	Expression C
$70 + q + 15 + 1$	$\dfrac{13 - x + 5}{3}$

Expression A	Expression A
$3 + d$	$33 + f$
Expression B	Expression B
$9y - 5$	$52 - a - 3$
Expression C	Expression C
$11.8 + i + 7$	$\dfrac{12x - 82}{5}$

Expression A	Expression A
$2p$	$10c$
Expression B	Expression B
$h - 3 + 2$	$5b + 2$
Expression C	Expression C
$5b + 2.7$	$12s + 2s + 10$

Expression A	Expression A
$9y$	$5b$
Expression B	Expression B
$y - 10 + 3$	$77 + f - 43$
Expression C	Expression C
$10 + r + 3.5$	$11e + 10 + 41$

Games Kit Resource Guide • Expression Expert Cards (1 of 4)

Expression Expert Cards

Expression A
$h - 3$

Expression B
$2p + 12$

Expression C
$\dfrac{14 + r + 3}{7}$

Expression A
$y - 10$

Expression B
$\dfrac{20}{f + 1}$

Expression C
$5 + 2y + 1.3$

Expression A
$\dfrac{20}{f}$

Expression B
$10c + 44$

Expression C
$8 + 2j - 22$

Expression A
$15 + j$

Expression B
$15 + j - 22$

Expression C
$12 - \dfrac{s + 2}{2}$

Expression A
$9 + a$

Expression B
$15 + g + 23$

Expression C
$\dfrac{15}{f + 17} - 8$

Expression A
$18 - s$

Expression B
$18 - s + 2$

Expression C
$(10c + 44) \times 5$

Expression A
$14 + r$

Expression B
$14 + r + 31$

Expression C
$3 + \dfrac{d - 2}{2}$

Expression A
$11 + q$

Expression B
$11 + q + 15$

Expression C
$(22 - y) - (5 \times 1y)$

Expression Expert Cards

Card 1
Expression A: $13 - x$
Expression B: $13 - x + 5$
Expression C: $\dfrac{25}{c+14}$

Card 2
Expression A: $10 + r$
Expression B: $10 + r + 3$
Expression C: $2m + 3m$

Card 3
Expression A: $7d$
Expression B: $7d + 15$
Expression C: $4h - 3h + 2$

Card 4
Expression A: $4b$
Expression B: $4b + 20$
Expression C: $9y - 4y + 7$

Card 5
Expression A: $9x$
Expression B: $9x + 16$
Expression C: $4b + 20 + 1b$

Card 6
Expression A: $11e$
Expression B: $11e + 10$
Expression C: $4h - 20 + 1.5h$

Card 7
Expression A: $\dfrac{25}{c}$
Expression B: $\dfrac{25}{c+14}$
Expression C: $\dfrac{50}{z-10+5z}$

Card 8
Expression A: $\dfrac{50}{z}$
Expression B: $\dfrac{50}{z-10}$
Expression C: $15 - 9 + a$

Expression Expert Cards

Expression A
$11 + i$

Expression B
$11 + i + 7$

Expression C
$77 + 7f - 4f$

Expression A
$\dfrac{15}{f}$

Expression B
$\dfrac{15}{f + 17}$

Expression C
$15 + g - 2g$

Expression A
$22 - y$

Expression B
$22 - y - 5$

Expression C
$52 - (10a \times 1.5)$

Expression A
$2m$

Expression B
$2m + 15$

Expression C
$3y - 20 + 3$

Expression A
$12 + s$

Expression B
$12 + s + 10$

Expression C
$7d + 15 - 3d$

Expression A
$4h$

Expression B
$4h - 20$

Expression C
$\dfrac{2p + 12}{2p}$

Expression A
$14 + v$

Expression B
$14 + v + 13$

Expression C
$8d - 50 + 2d$

Expression A
$8d$

Expression B
$8d - 50$

Expression C
$9x + 16 + 12$

Ratio Fishing Cards

C1 Karen's fruit punch recipe uses 4 cups of pineapple juice for every 2 cups of apple juice. How much pineapple juice will Karen use if she uses only 1 cup of apple juice?

C2 Yukiri walked at a constant speed and traveled 6 miles in 3 hours. What was Yukiri's speed in miles per hour?

C3 Garrett is selling lemonade. He sold 9 liters of lemonade in 3 hours. How many liters, on average, did he sell per hour?

C4 Isaac used 12 tablespoons of butter to make 4 loaves of bread. How many tablespoons of butter are needed to make 1 loaf of bread?

C5 Daniel and his team built 12 tables in 3 weeks. How many tables did they build per week?

C6 The class sold 32 boxes of snack bars in 8 weeks of fundraising. How many boxes of snack bars did the class sell per week?

C7 A basketball player scored 18 points in 6 minutes. How many points did she average per minute?

C8 A 4.5 pound block of cheese costs $22.50. What is the price for one pound of cheese?

Ratio Fishing Cards

C9 If Matthew uses 10 tablespoons of coffee to fill his 5 cup coffee maker, how much would he need to make one cup of coffee?

C10 The school gathered 14 pallets of food for the food bank in 7 weeks. How many pallets of food did the school gather per week?

C11 Jake walked around a track at a constant speed. He walked $2\frac{1}{4}$ miles in $\frac{3}{4}$ hours. What was Jake's speed in miles per hour?

C12 Isaac used $\frac{1}{4}$ of a cup of nuts to fill $\frac{1}{12}$ of a container. How many cups of nuts are needed to fill the entire container?

C13 Sasha took 25 pictures in $6\frac{1}{4}$ minutes. How many pictures did Sasha take per minute?

C14 Alicia jogged at a constant speed and traveled 7 miles in $1\frac{3}{4}$ hours. What was Alicia's speed in miles per hour?

C15 Ron is selling water at the fair. He sold $1\frac{1}{4}$ liters of water every $\frac{1}{4}$ hour. How many liters did he sell in one hour?

C16 47.5 gallons of water drained out of a bathtub in 9.5 minutes. How many gallons of water drained each minute?

Ratio Fishing Cards

C17 Alejandro spent $11.25 for 22.5 pounds of potatoes. What was the cost per pound?

C18 The basketball teams ordered pizzas. If the 25 players ate $12\frac{1}{2}$ pizzas, how much of a pizza, on average, did each player eat?

C19 Petra used $\frac{1}{9}$ of a pound of nuts to make $\frac{1}{3}$ of a recipe for trail mix. How many pounds of nuts are needed to make a whole recipe of trail mix?

C20 After a game, 4 bottles of sports drinks were poured into cups for 12 players to drink. How much sports drink did each player get?

C21 Rachelle used $\frac{1}{8}$ tsp of salt for a $\frac{1}{2}$ batch of bread. How much salt does she need for a full batch of bread?

C22 Ben used $2\frac{2}{3}$ cups of granola to make a $\frac{2}{3}$ batch of snack bars. How much granola does he need for a full batch of snack bars?

C23 Anna can install 4 shelves in 20 minutes. How many shelves can Anna install per minute?

C24 The debate team ate $1\frac{2}{5}$ platters of sandwiches among the 7 team members. How much of the sandwich platter, on average, did each team member eat?

Ratio Fishing Cards

C25 Carlita used $\frac{1}{4}$ cup of flour for a $\frac{1}{2}$ batch of pancakes. How much flour does she need for a full batch of pancakes?

C26 The 15 members of a soccer team ate 7.5 pizzas. How much of a pizza, on average, did each team member eat?

C27 Denny used 7 ounces of jam to make 21 sandwiches. How much jam did he use per sandwich?

C28 Fara can paint $1\frac{1}{3}$ fence panels in 4 hours. How much of a fence panel can Fara paint per hour?

C29 Greta was charged $3.75 for 15 granola bites. What was the cost of each granola bite?

C30 Hannah used 5 liters of soap to wash 20 cars. How much of a liter of soap was needed for each car?

C31 15 friends shared 3 pizzas. How much pizza, on average, did each friend get?

C32 Jacalyn planted $1\frac{2}{3}$ acres of crops in $8\frac{1}{3}$ hours. How much of an acre, on average, did she plant per hour?

Ratio Fishing Cards

C33 Keisha and her friend earned $54 for doing $4\frac{1}{2}$ hours of yard work. How much did they earn each hour?

C34 Isaiah biked at a constant speed and traveled 27 miles in $2\frac{1}{4}$ hours. What was Isaiah's speed in miles per hour?

C35 Laura scored 84 points after playing 7 levels in a video game. How many points did she earn, on average, per level?

C36 114 gallons of water drained out of a holding tank in $9\frac{1}{2}$ minutes. How many gallons of water drained each minute?

C37 Malik memorized $3\frac{3}{4}$ pages of sheet music in 5 hours. How many pages, on average, did he memorize per hour?

C38 Natalie cleaned $1\frac{1}{8}$ miles of beach in $1\frac{1}{2}$ hours. How many miles did she clean per hour?

C39 8 friends shared 6 calzones. How much of a calzone, on average, did each friend eat?

C40 Odell used $\frac{3}{8}$ teaspoon of vanilla to make a $\frac{1}{2}$ batch of yogurt. How much vanilla does he need to make a full batch of yogurt?

Ratio Fishing Cards

C41	C42
8 : 4	20 : 10

C43	C44
15 : 5	9 : 3

C45	C46
8 : 2	20 : 5

C47	C48
20 : 4	10 : 2

Ratio Fishing Cards

C49 100 students in 10 classrooms	**C50** 50 miles in 10 hours
C51 60 cups for 6 parties	**C52** 40 cups for 10 tables
C53 30 miles in 2 hours	**C54** 60 pages in 4 days
C55 90 apples in 6 bags	**C56** 105 tickets sold in 7 days

Ratio Fishing Cards Answer Key

C1. 2	C25. $\frac{1}{2}$	C41. 2
C2. 2	C26. $\frac{1}{2}$	C42. 2
C3. 3	C27. $\frac{1}{3}$	C43. 3
C4. 3	C28. $\frac{1}{3}$	C44. 3
C5. 4	C29. $\frac{1}{4}$	C45. 4
C6. 4	C30. $\frac{1}{4}$	C46. 4
C7. 3	C31. $\frac{1}{5}$	C47. 5
C8. 5	C32. $\frac{1}{5}$	C48. 5
C9. 2	C33. 12	C49. 10
C10. 2	C34. 12	C50. 5
C11. 3	C35. 12	C51. 10
C12. 3	C36. 12	C52. 4
C13. 4	C37. $\frac{3}{4}$	C53. 15
C14. 4	C38. $\frac{3}{4}$	C54. 15
C15. 5	C39. $\frac{3}{4}$	C55. 15
C16. 5	C40. $\frac{3}{4}$	C56. 15
C17. $\frac{1}{2}$		
C18. $\frac{1}{2}$		
C19. $\frac{1}{3}$		
C20. $\frac{1}{3}$		
C21. $\frac{1}{4}$		
C22. $\frac{1}{4}$		
C23. $\frac{1}{5}$		
C24. $\frac{1}{5}$		

Ratio Fishing Record Sheet

Card #	Unit Rate	Card #	Unit Rate
C____		C____	
C____		C____	
C____		C____	
C____		C____	
C____		C____	
C____		C____	
C____		C____	
C____		C____	

Architectural Blueprints

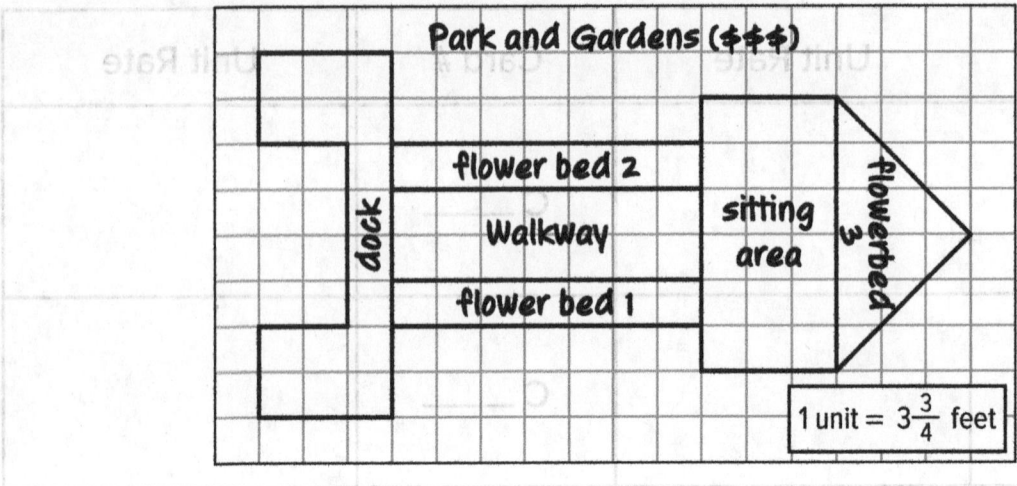

150 Architectural Blueprints (1 of 2) • **Games Kit Resource Guide**

Architectural Blueprints

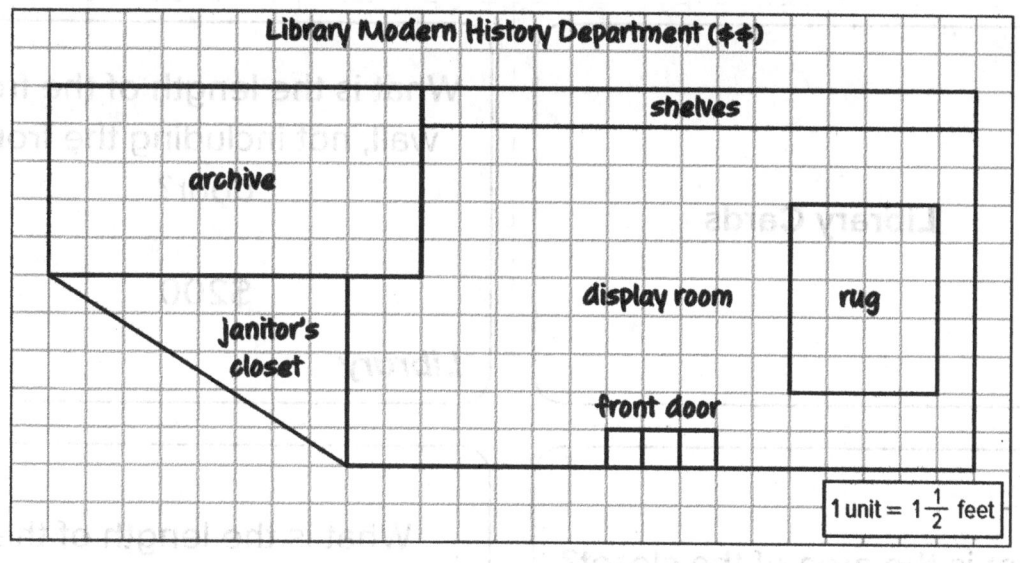

Job Site Cards

Library Cards

What is the length of the front wall, not including the front door?

$200

Library

What is the area of the closet?

$600

Library

What is the length of the shelves on the back wall?

$100

Library

What is the perimeter of the archive room?

$300

Library

What are the dimensions of the rug in the display room?

$200

Library

What is the area of the display room, not including the shelves?

$600

Library

What is the area of the archive room?

$300

Library

Job Site Cards

Park and Garden Cards

What is the total area of all 3 flower beds?

$600

Park and Garden

What is the area of the dock?

$500

Park and Garden

What is the area of flower bed 2?

$100

Park and Garden

What is the perimeter of the dock?

$400

Park and Garden

What is the perimeter of flower bed 3?

$600

Park and Garden

What is the area of flower bed 1?

$100

Park and Garden

What are the dimensions of the sitting area?

$300

Park and Garden

Job Site Cards

Subway Cards	What is the perimeter of platform 2? $300 *Subway*
What is the total area of both platforms, including the bathrooms? $300 *Subway*	What is the total area of all escalators? $400 *Subway*
What is the total area of both bathrooms? $100 *Subway*	What is the length of platform 1? $100 *Subway*
What is the area of platform 1, not including the bathroom? $300 *Subway*	What is the perimeter of one of the bathrooms? $200 *Subway*

Job Site Cards

Skate Park Cards

What is the area of the grind rails section?

$500

Skate Park

What is the area of the entire park?

$300

Skate Park

What is the perimeter of the entire park?

$400

Skate Park

What are the dimensions of the half pipe section?

$200

Skate Park

What is the length of the large grind rail?

$100

Skate Park

What is the area of the quarter pipe section?

$200

Skate Park

What is the total area of the grind rails and the flat bank ramp sections?

$600

Skate Park

Circle Circuits Record Sheet

$$A = \pi r^2$$
$$C = 2\pi r$$

Orange Circuit

Area = _____

Circumference = _____

Purple Circuit

Area = _____

Circumference = _____

Blue Circuit

Area = _____

Circumference = _____

Yellow Circuit

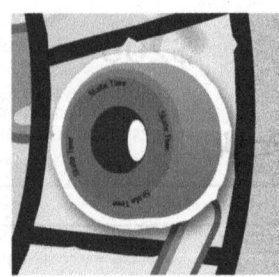

Area = _____

Circumference = _____

Population Cards

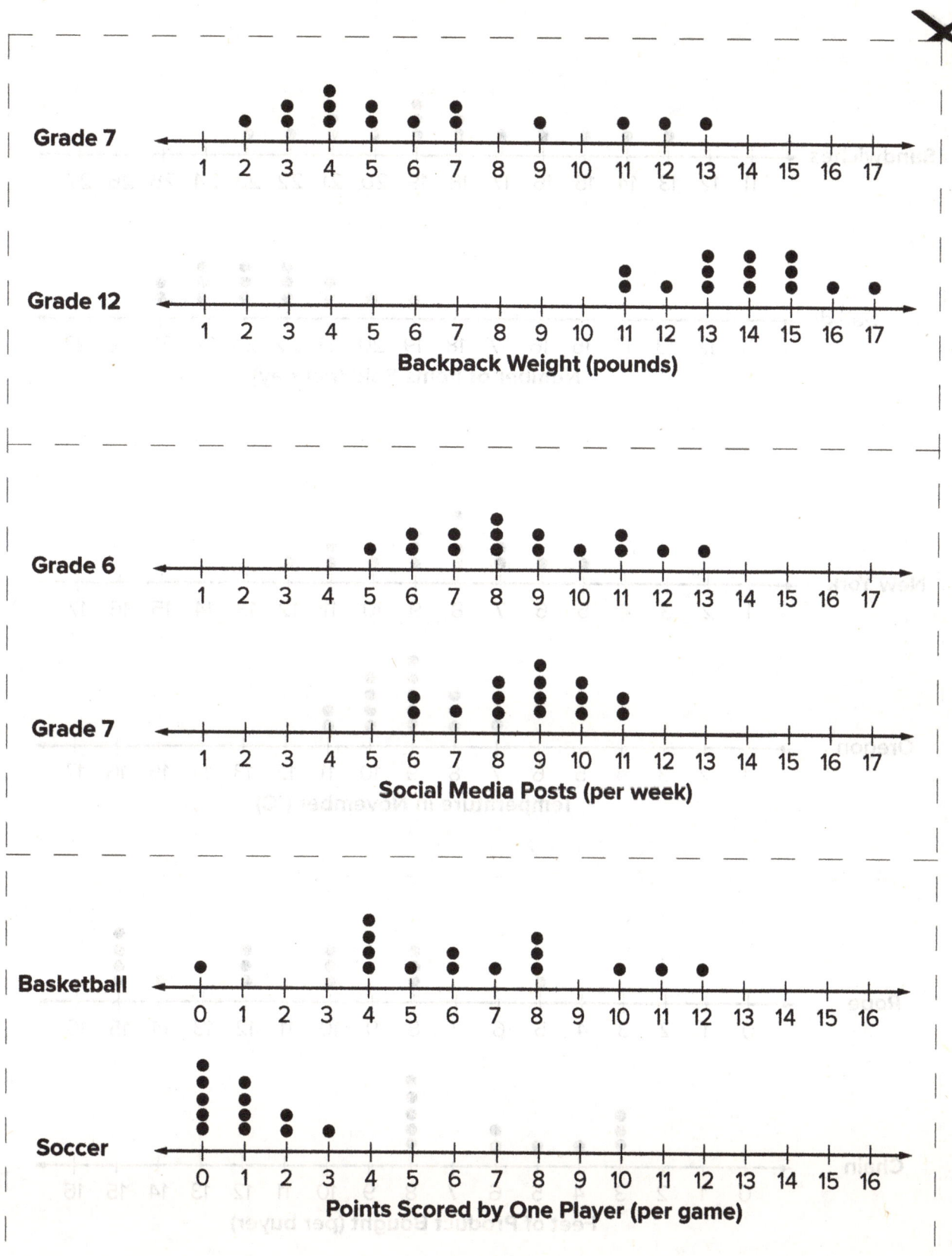

Games Kit Resource Guide • Population Cards (1 of 9)

Population Cards

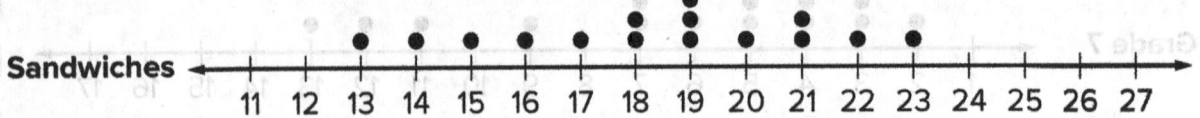
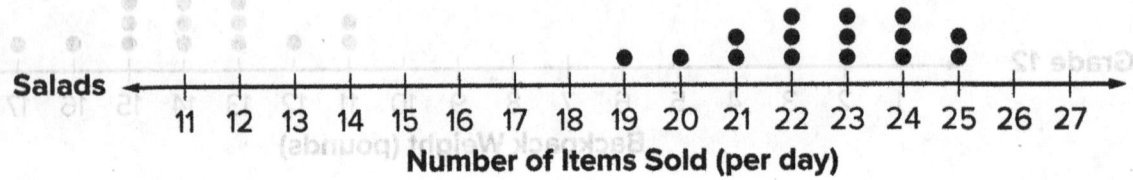

Number of Items Sold (per day)

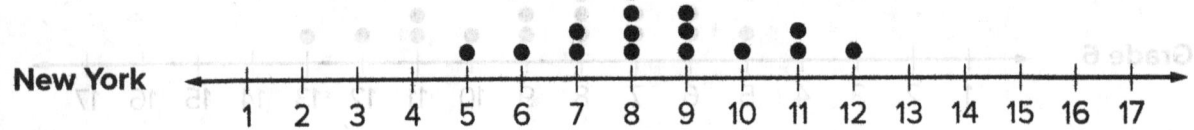
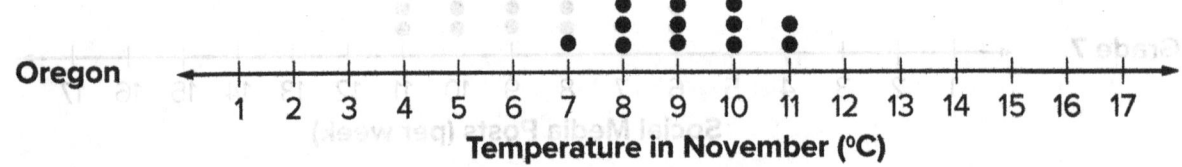

Temperature in November (°C)

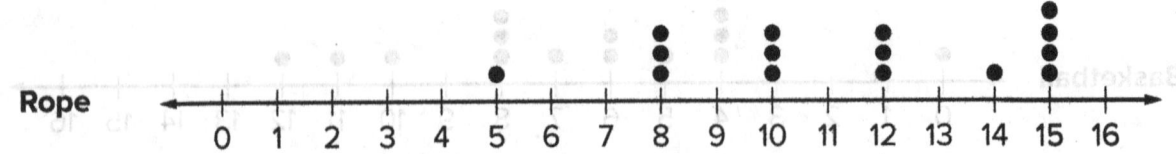
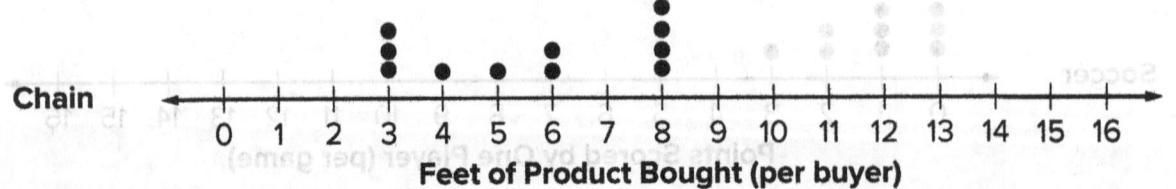

Feet of Product Bought (per buyer)

Population Cards

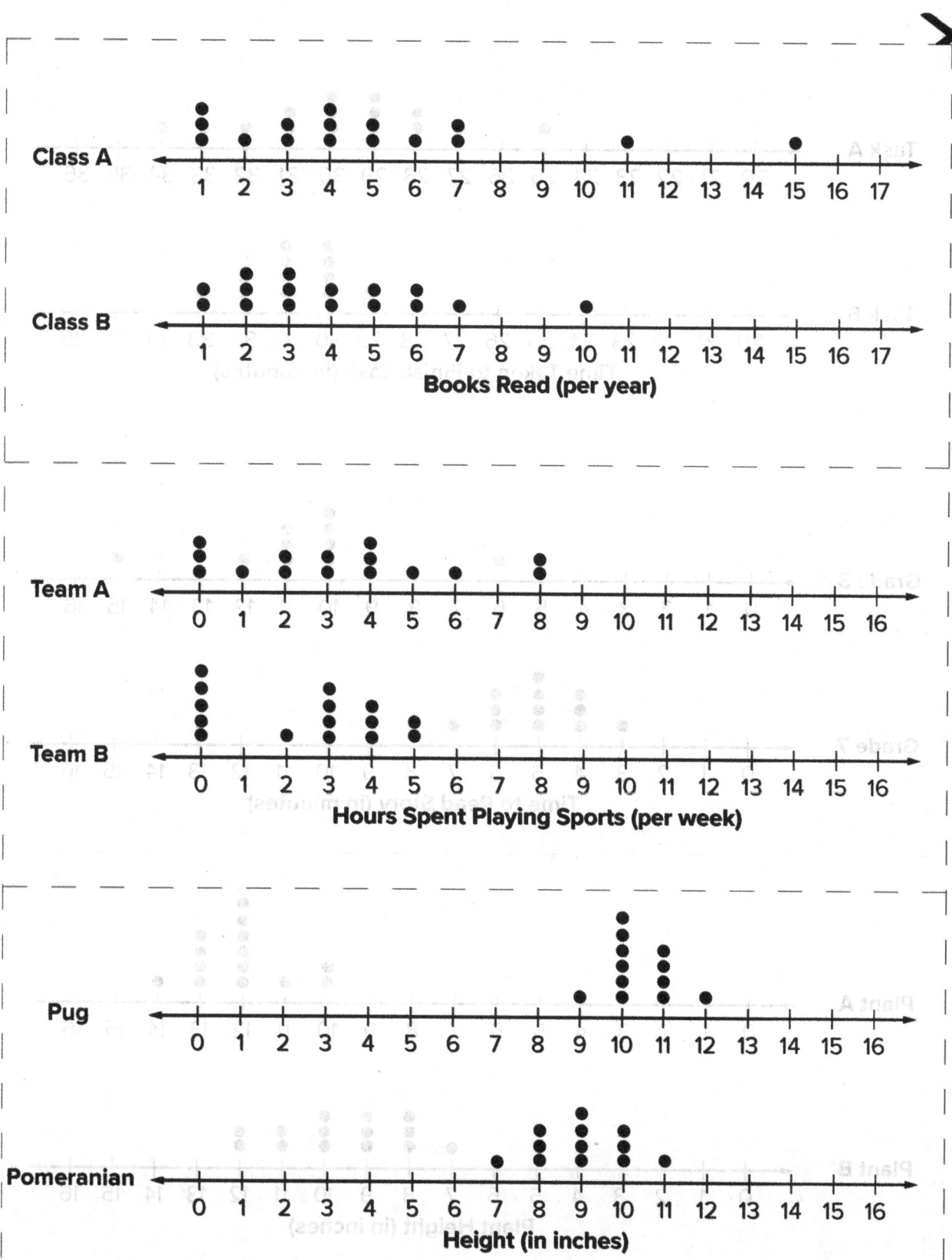

Population Cards

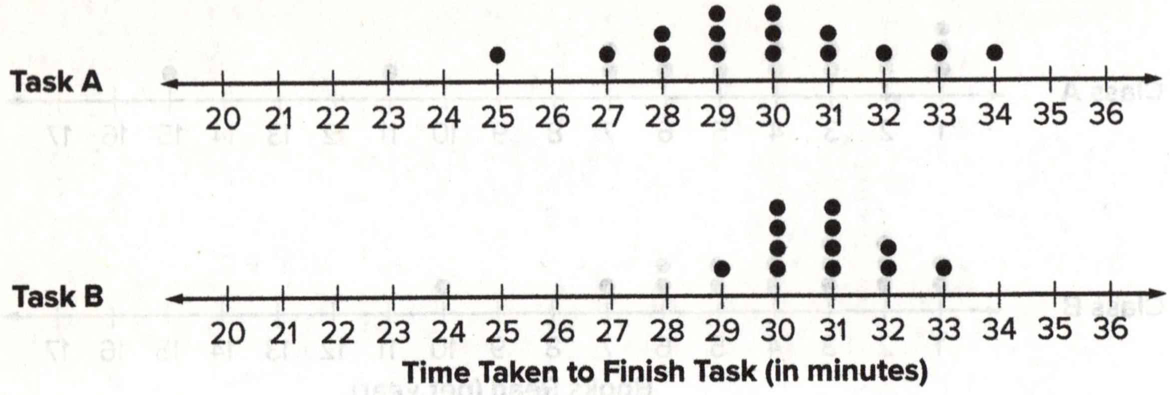

Task A — dot plot, x-axis: 20 21 22 23 24 25 26 27 28 29 30 31 32 33 34 35 36
- 25: 1
- 27: 2
- 28: 3
- 29: 4
- 30: 4
- 31: 3
- 32: 2
- 33: 2
- 34: 1

Task B — dot plot, x-axis: 20 21 22 23 24 25 26 27 28 29 30 31 32 33 34 35 36
- 29: 1
- 30: 4
- 31: 4
- 32: 2
- 33: 1

Time Taken to Finish Task (in minutes)

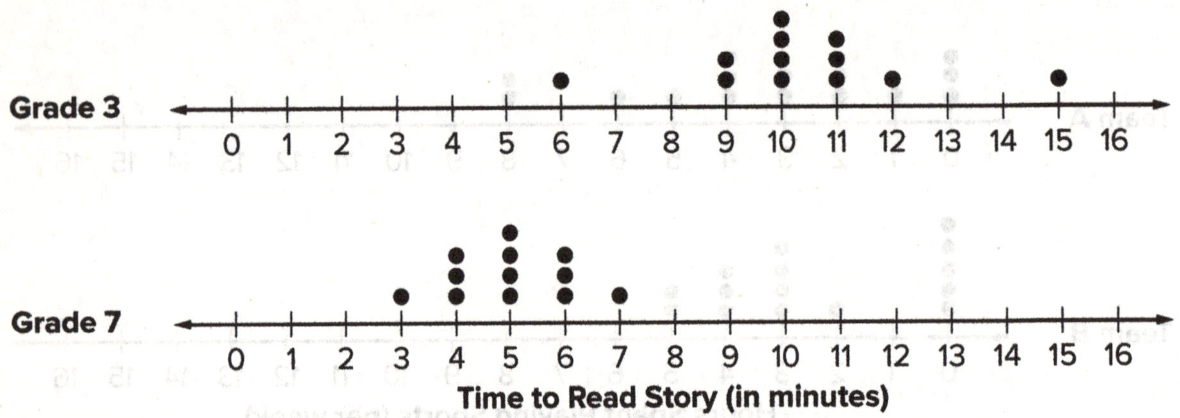

Grade 3 — dot plot, x-axis: 0–16
- 6: 1
- 9: 2
- 10: 3
- 11: 2
- 12: 1
- 15: 1

Grade 7 — dot plot, x-axis: 0–16
- 3: 1
- 4: 3
- 5: 4
- 6: 3
- 7: 1

Time to Read Story (in minutes)

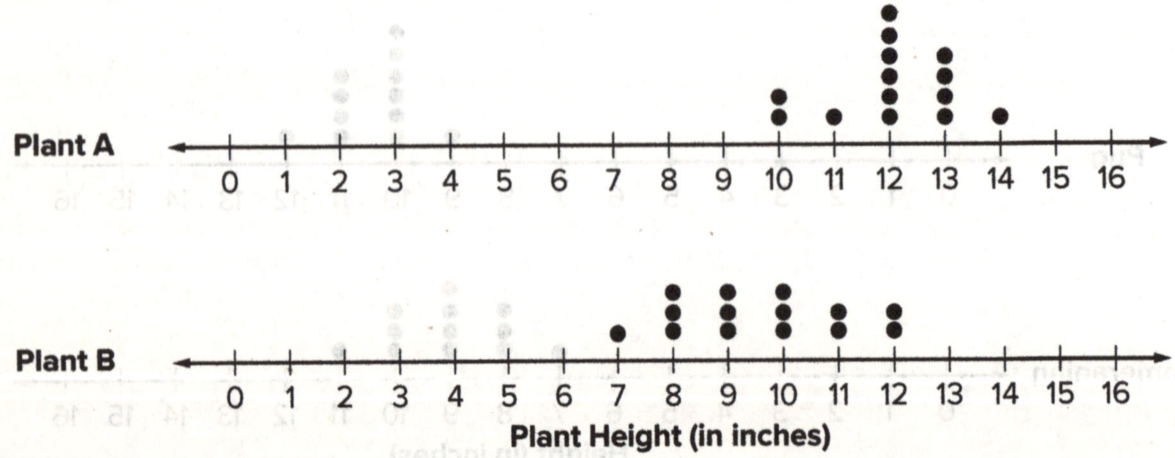

Plant A — dot plot, x-axis: 0–16
- 10: 2
- 11: 1
- 12: 4
- 13: 3
- 14: 1

Plant B — dot plot, x-axis: 0–16
- 7: 1
- 8: 3
- 9: 3
- 10: 3
- 11: 2
- 12: 2

Plant Height (in inches)

Population Cards

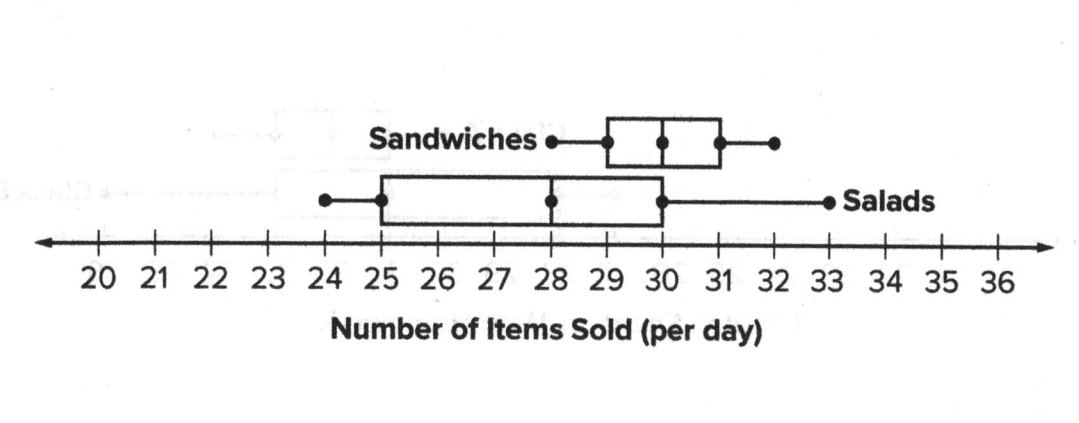

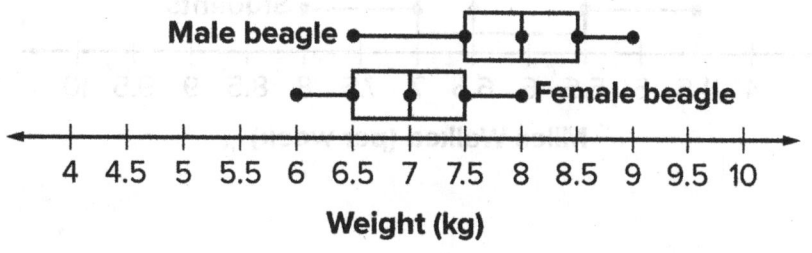

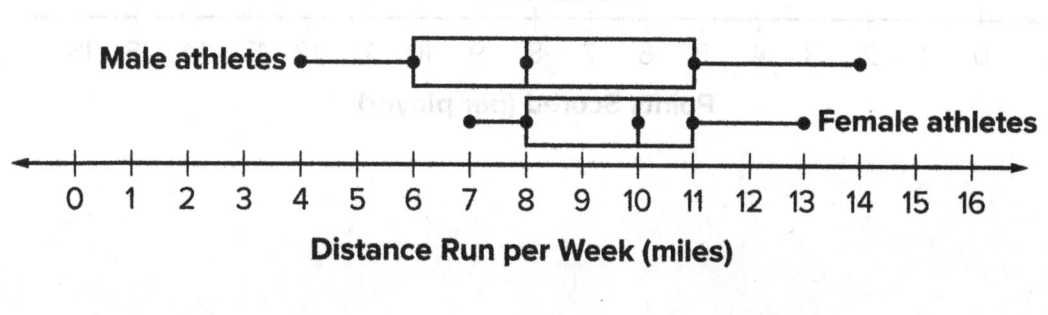

Population Cards

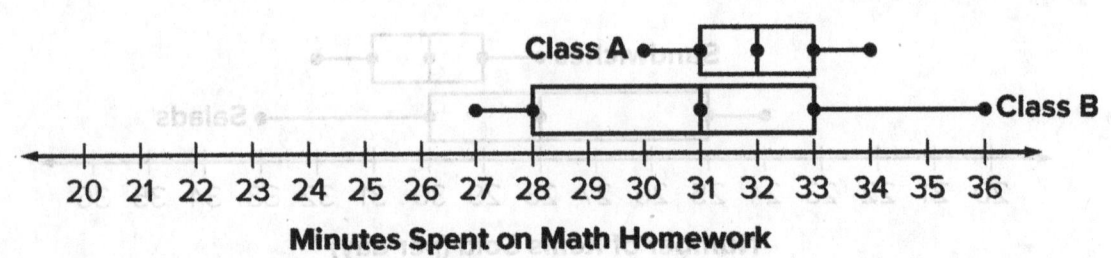

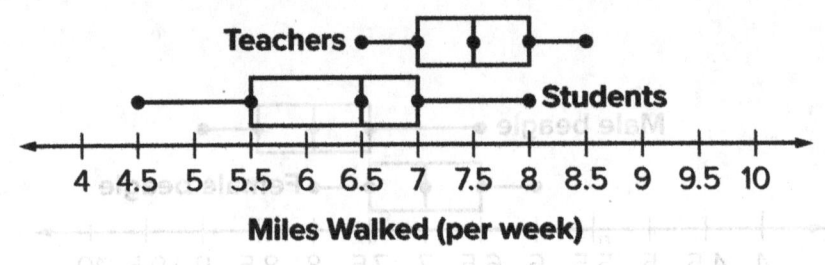

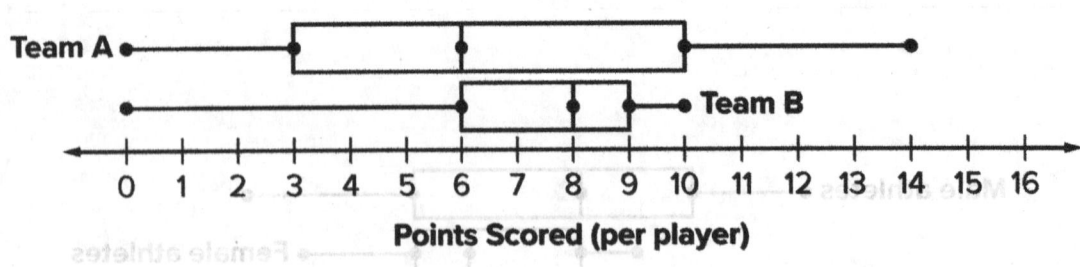

Population Cards

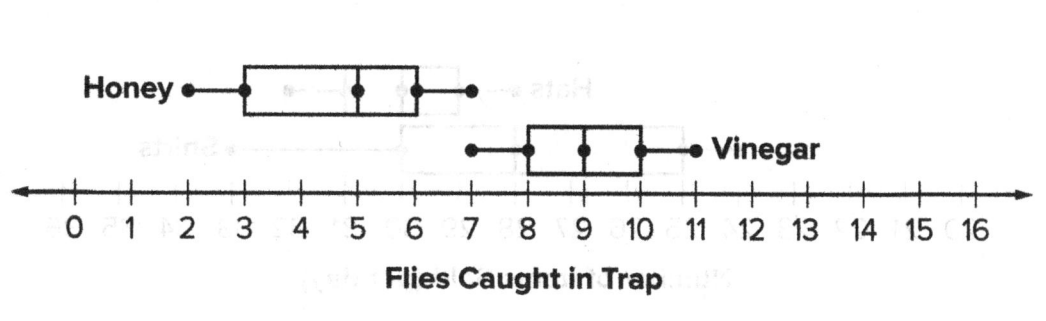

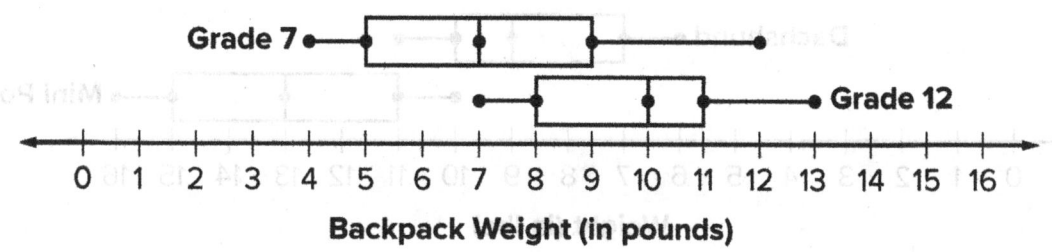

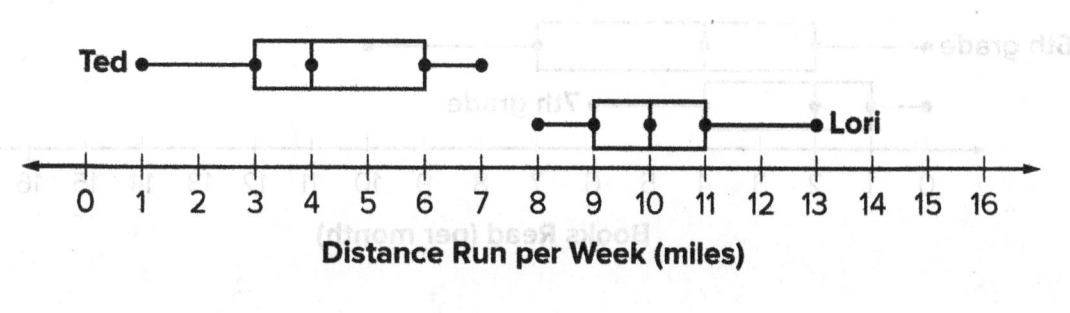

Population Cards

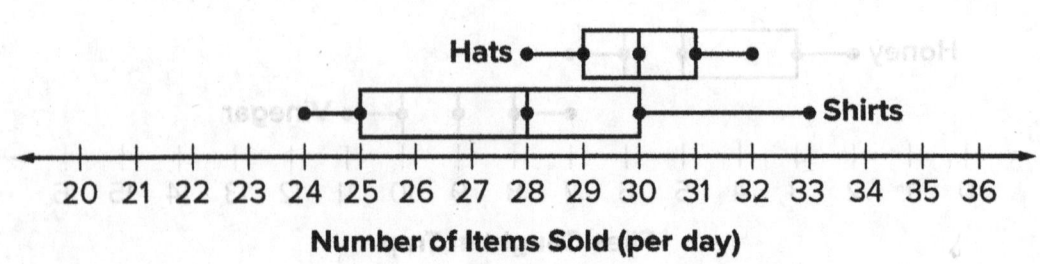

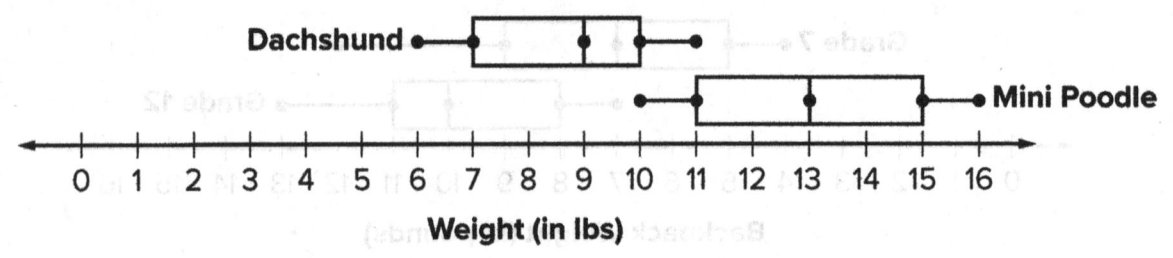

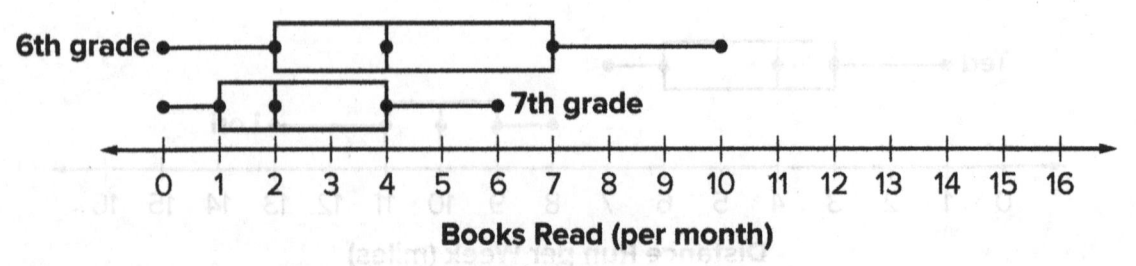

Population Cards Answer Key

Dot Plots

Lesser Median	Greater Median	Lesser Range	Greater Range
Grade 7	Grade 12	Grade 12	Grade 7
Grade 6	Grade 7	Grade 7	Grade 6
Soccer	Basketball	Soccer	Basketball
Sandwiches	Salads	Salads	Sandwiches
New York	Oregon	Oregon	New York
Chain	Rope	Chain	Rope
Class B	Class A	Class B	Class A
same	same	Team B	Team A
Pomeranian	Pug	Pug	Pomeranian
Task A	Task B	Task B	Task A
Grade 7	Grade 3	Grade 7	Grade 3
Plant B	Plant A	Plant A	Plant B

Box Plots

Lesser Median	Greater Median	Lesser Range	Greater Range
Salads	Sandwiches	Sandwiches	Salads
Female beagle	Male beagle	Female beagle	Male beagle
Male athletes	Female athletes	Female athletes	Male athletes
Class B	Class A	Class A	Class B
Students	Teachers	Teachers	Students
Team A	Team B	Team B	Team A
Honey	Vinegar	Vinegar	Honey
Grade 7	Grade 12	Grade 12	Grade 7
Ted	Lori	Lori	Ted
Shirts	Hats	Hats	Shirts
Dachshund	Mini Poodle	Dachshund	Mini Poodle
7th grade	6th grade	7th grade	6th grade

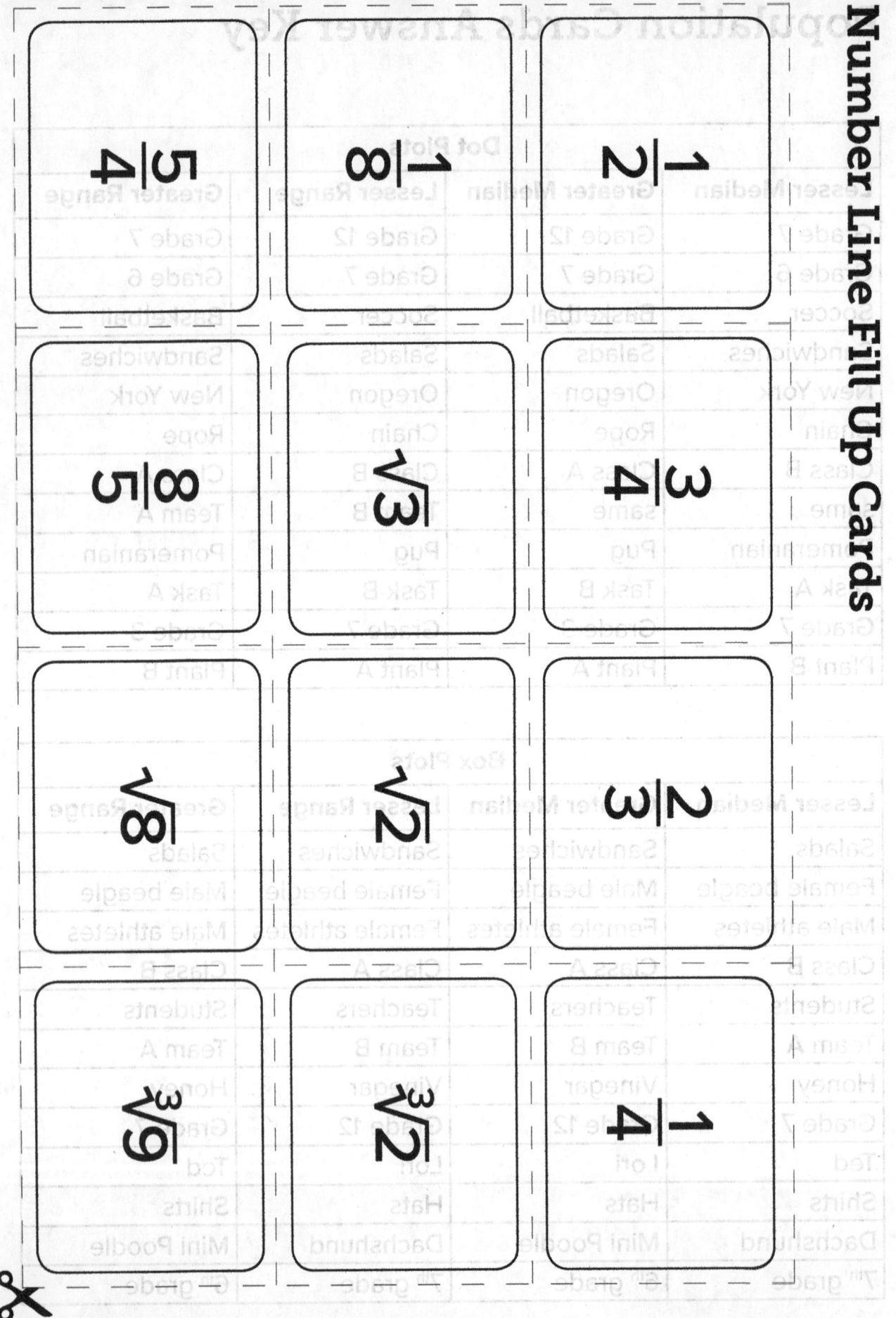

Number Line Fill Up Cards

$\sqrt{13}$	$\sqrt[3]{29}$	$\sqrt[3]{65}$
$\sqrt{6}$	$\dfrac{15}{4}$	$\dfrac{9}{2}$
$\dfrac{9}{4}$	$\dfrac{10}{3}$	$\dfrac{13}{3}$
$\dfrac{7}{3}$	$\sqrt[3]{45}$	$\sqrt[3]{100}$

Number Line Fill Up Cards

$\sqrt[3]{300}$	$\sqrt[3]{135}$	$\sqrt{20}$
$\dfrac{13}{2}$	$\sqrt{27}$	$\dfrac{11}{2}$
$\dfrac{19}{3}$	$\sqrt{43}$	$\dfrac{31}{6}$
$\sqrt{40}$	$\sqrt[3]{250}$	$\sqrt[3]{150}$

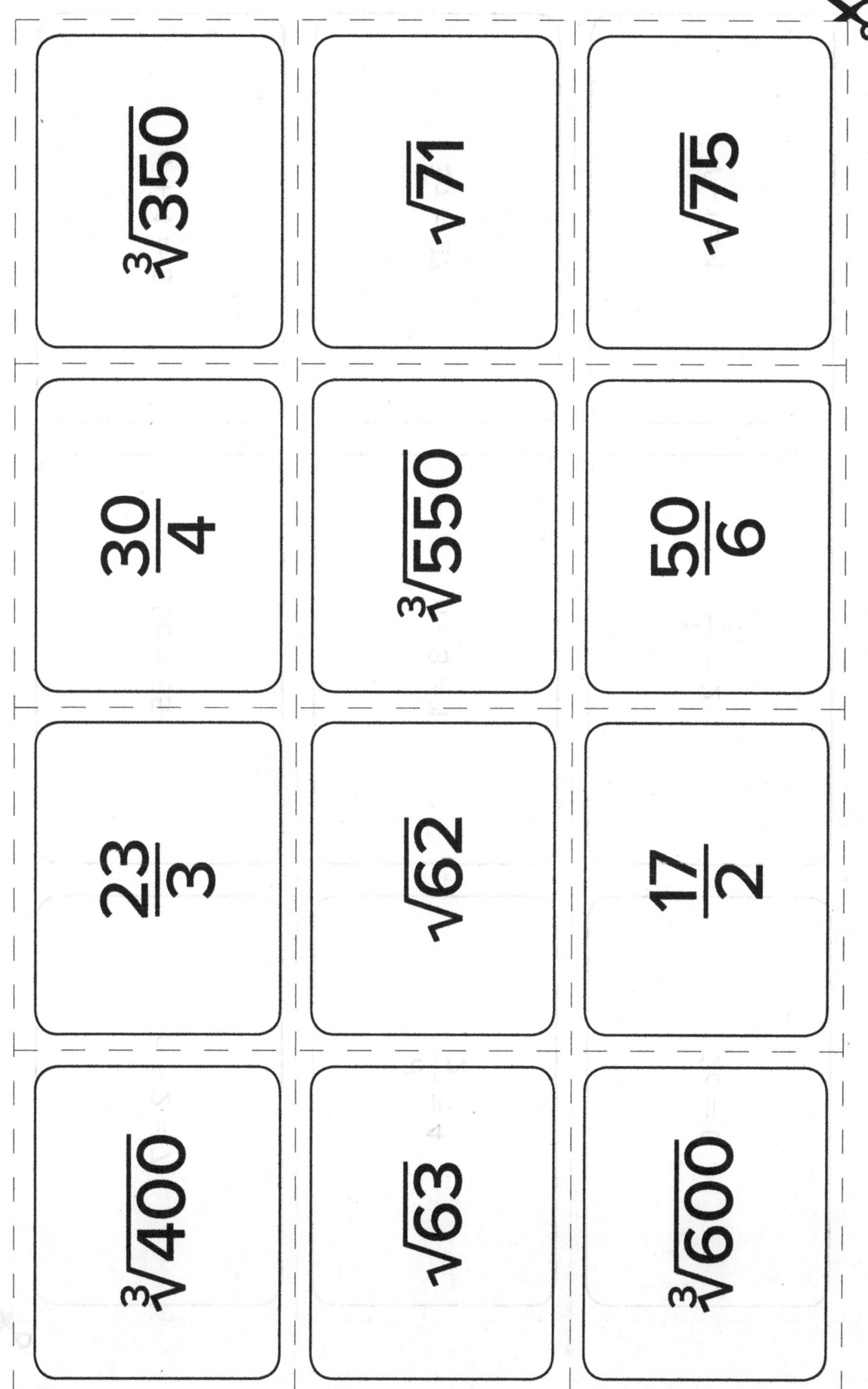

Linear Equation Cards

- $a + 4 = 5$
- $3a = 27$
- $f - 1 = 1$

- $5c = 35$
- $d - 3 = 1$
- $\dfrac{f}{3} = 2$

- $c + 2 = 7$
- $\dfrac{d}{2} = 4$
- $2c = 6$

Linear Equation Cards

$a + 4 = 3$	$-4c = 24$	$c + 7 = 2$
$12a = -24$	$d + 3 = 1$	$f - 1 = -5$
$\dfrac{d}{3} = -3$	$\dfrac{j}{5} = -2$	$-2c = 6$

Linear Equation Cards

$c + 7 = 9$	$8g = -16$	$f - 3 = 1$
$4a = 28$	$d - 6 = 2$	$\dfrac{f}{3} = 1$
$c + 5 = 2$	$f - 2 = -6$	$-2d = 16$

Linear Equation Cards

$4m = -m + 5$	$7h = 4h + 24$	$g - 24 = 5g$
$10 = 2f - 4$	$\dfrac{3g}{5} = -3$	$2(5j) = 50$
$2a + 2 = 12$	$4g - 3 = g$	$3(2c) = 24$

Linear Equation Cards

$2a + 4 = 12$	$3h + 4 = 2h - 5$	$6r + 2 = 5r - 4$
$a + 20 = 3a$	$\dfrac{2b}{8} = 1$	$\dfrac{d + 30}{3} = 9$
$3g + 3 = -6$	$\dfrac{c + 3}{2} = 5$	$a - 8 = 3a$

Linear Equation Cards

$3a + 5 = 17$	$2d + 15 = 5d$	$2g - 10 = 6$
$4h - 4 = 5h + 3$	$\dfrac{3b}{2} = b + 4$	$\dfrac{f-4}{2} = -5$
$6r + 5 = 5r + 3$	$\dfrac{m+12}{2} = 8$	$5h + 12 = 2h$

Linear Equation Cards

- $2d + 9 = 5d$
- $4x + 3 = 3x - 5$
- $2x - 4 = -10$

- $-17 = 3x + 4$
- $\dfrac{d+12}{5} = 2$
- $\dfrac{d+5}{3} = 5$

- $4m = m - 6$
- $7x = 2(3x - 3)$
- $5(a - 1) = -45$

Linear Equation Cards

$4(v+2) = -3(2v+5) + 3$	$5k + 4 - 2k = 2(k+3)$	$4m + 8 - 2m = 3(m+4)$
$2 - 4(d+3) = -d + 5$	$2(h+9) = 3(h+2)$	$2x + 5 = \dfrac{3(x+4)}{6}$
$v + 2(v+3) = 6(v+5)$	$12 - 4(d+3) = d - 5$	$2(d+5) - 3 = 33 - (5+d)$

Function Cards

Carrie had $3 in her change box. She earned $1 for every cup of lemonade she sold.

Daniel makes balloon animals at the fair. He made 2 animals. Then he made 2 more animals every hour.

The water was 5°C. Every minute the temperature of the water increased by 3°C.

x	0	1	2	3
y	6	7	8	9

x	0	1	2	3
y	3	5	7	9

x	0	2	4	6
y	1	7	13	19

$y - x = -3$

$y + 5 = 2x$

$y = 3x$

Function Cards

$y = 4x$	$y = 5x - 2$	$y = 6x - 1$

x	−2	−1	0	1
y	−2	2	6	10

x	−2	−1	0	1
y	−10	−5	0	5

x	0	2	4	6
y	5	17	29	41

Julie owned 3 books. She then bought 4 books per week.

Natalie found 7 colored pencils. Each day she found 5 more pencils for her collection.

Petra did not sell any bagels in the morning at the deli. In the afternoon, Petra sells 6 bagels per hour.

Function Cards

$y = 7x - 2$

$y = 8x - 12$

$y = 9x - 5$

x	0	1	2	3
y	0	7	14	21

x	0	1	2	3
y	3	11	19	27

x	-1	0	1	2
y	-2	7	16	25

Emily had 3 tennis balls. She bought 7 more tennis balls each week.

Oran had $5 in his bank account. He earned $8 for each lawn that he cut.

Maryanne had 3 picture frames already made. She then made 9 picture frames per week.

Function Cards

Kelsea made 10 bracelets. Each day she gives one bracelet to a friend.	Yuri had $9 in his bank account. Every day he spent $2.	Mack had $4 in credit at the store. He then spent $3 per day at the store.

x	0	1	2	3
y	6	5	4	3

x	0	1	2	3
y	10	8	6	4

x	−3	−2	−1	0
y	10	7	4	1

$-8 - y = -x$

$-7 - y = -2x$

$-10 + y = -3x$

Games Kit Resource Guide • Function Cards (4 of 6) **181**

Function Cards

$y = -4x + 11$

$y = -5x + 10$

$y = -6x + 4$

x	-2	0	2	4
y	17	12	7	2

x	-2	0	2	4
y	17	12	7	2

x	1	2	3	4
y	11	5	-1	-7

Abigail has a credit of 12 items on her store account. Every week she buys 4 items.

The temperature of the liquid was 7°C. Every hour the temperature dropped by 5°C.

The liquid was 7°F. The temperature of the liquid dropped 6 degrees per hour.

Function Cards

The metal ball was on the surface of the water. Every second the ball sinks 7 feet.	The hiker was 10 feet above sea level. Every minute she hikes 8 feet down.	The store started the month with $0. Each day they lost $9 in product from damage.

x	1	2	3	4
y	2	−5	−18	−25

x	−3	−2	−1	0
y	12	4	−4	−12

x	0	1	2	3
y	13	4	−5	−14

$y = -7x + 3$	$y = -8x + 1$	$y = -9x + 5$

Turn Up the Volume Sheet

Three-Dimensional Shape	Dimensions	Volume
Sphere $V = \frac{4}{3}\pi r^3$	Radius = _____	
Cylinder $V = \pi r^2 h$	Radius = _____ Height = _____	
Cone $V = \frac{1}{3}\pi r^2 h$	Radius = _____ Height = _____	

Extras (if needed)

Three-Dimensional Shape	Dimensions	Volume
Sphere $V = \frac{4}{3}\pi r^3$	Radius = _____	
Cylinder $V = \pi r^2 h$	Radius = _____ Height = _____	
Cone $V = \frac{1}{3}\pi r^2 h$	Radius = _____ Height = _____	

Add the volume of one of each shape. _____ + _____ + _____ = _____

    sphere   cylinder   cone   total

Transformation Cards with Triangles

| Rotation 90° Clockwise | Vertical Translation 3 units | Vertical Translation 3 units |

| Vertical Translation 3 units | Horizontal Translation 3 units | Horizontal Translation 3 units |

| Horizontal Translation 3 units | Rotation 90° Counter-Clockwise | Rotation 180° Clockwise |

Transformation Cards with Triangles

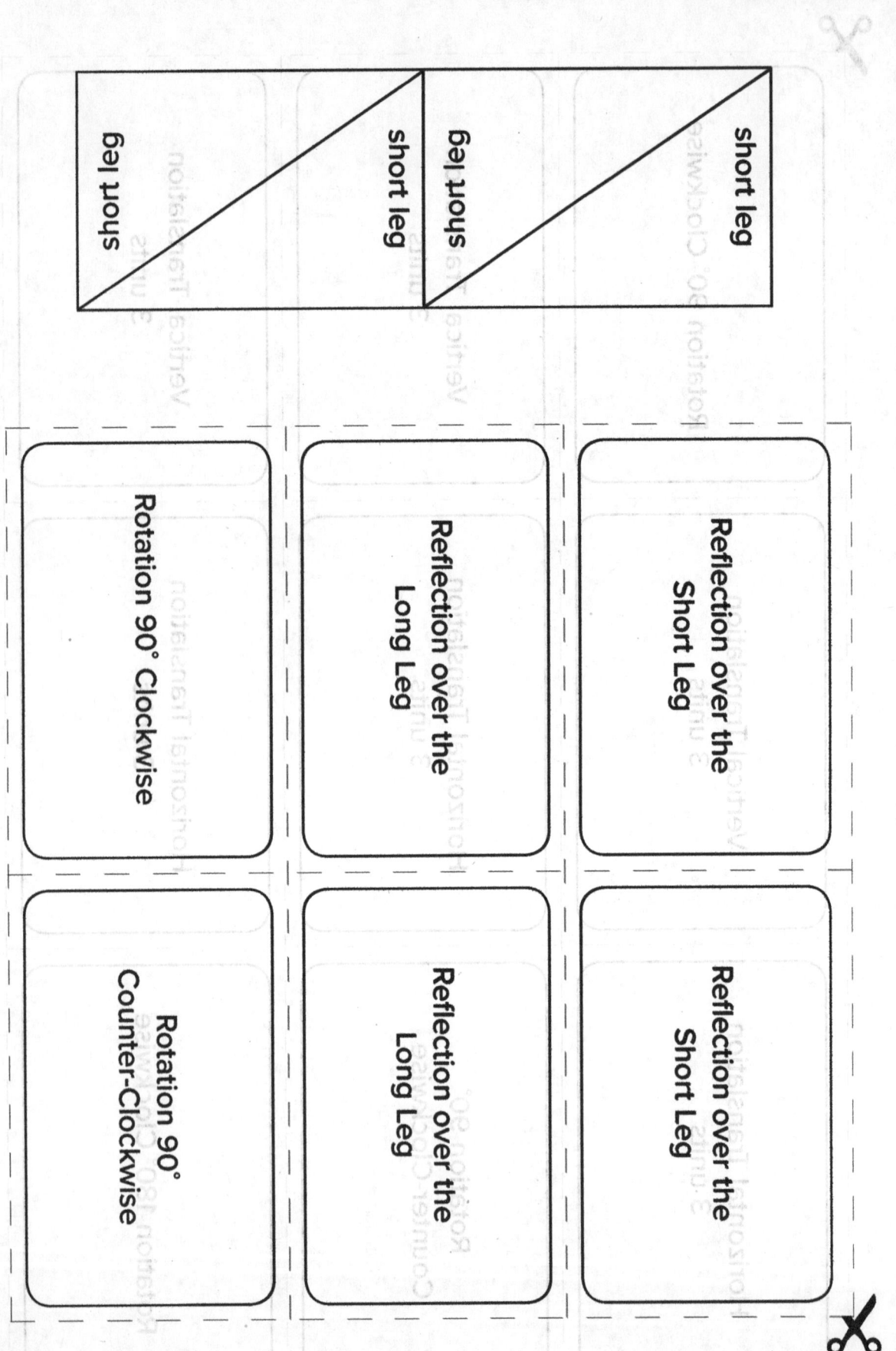

186 Transformation Cards with Triangles (2 of 2) • Games Kit Resource Guide

Coordinate Cards

(0,0) (5,2) (7,3) (8,4) (6,2) (2,1) (3,1) (8,3) positive association	(2,5) (1,2) (3,7) (2,6) (0,0) (1,3) (2,3) (3,8) positive association
(4,3) (5,6) (1,1) (5,5) (7,7) (0,0) (3,3) (8,8) positive association	(5,4) (0,1) (1,2) (7,6) (3,3) (2,2) (6,5) (4,3) positive association
(0,5) (4,6) (7,7) (5,7) (2,6) (3,6) (8,8) (1,5) positive association	(0,2) (2,6) (1,3) (3,6) (2,7) (3,8) (1,5) (1,4) positive association

Coordinate Cards

| (6, 2) (3, 5)
(7, 2) (5, 4)
(2, 6) (1, 7)
(5, 3) (7, 1)

negative association |

| (2, 2) (4, 1)
(3, 1) (0, 2)
(5, 1) (7, 0)
(8, 0) (6, 1)

negative association |

| (2, 5) (3, 4)
(0, 8) (1, 7)
(1, 6) (4, 2)
(4, 3) (5, 1)

negative association |

| (5, 2) (6, 1)
(6, 2) (4, 3)
(1, 5) (4, 2)
(2, 4) (3, 4)

negative association |

| (7, 3) (6, 4)
(2, 4) (1, 5)
(8, 3) (3, 4)
(0, 5) (5, 4)

negative association |

| (5, 4) (8, 3)
(3, 5) (0, 7)
(4, 5) (2, 6)
(7, 4) (6, 4)

negative association |

Coordinate Cards

(4 , 2) (7 , 2) (5 , 7) (1 , 5) (4 , 5) (7 , 5) (3 , 8) (1 , 7) no association	(7 , 1) (6 , 6) (2 , 1) (4 , 2) (7 , 4) (6 , 3) (2 , 3) (4 , 4) no association
(4 , 7) (4 , 3) (1 , 1) (8 , 6) (7 , 4) (4 , 4) (1 , 4) (7 , 5) no association	(6 , 3) (5 , 6) (2 , 7) (4 , 7) (6 , 7) (5 , 4) (3 , 3) (3 , 6) no association
(5 , 2) (6 , 7) (7 , 6) (5 , 6) (8 , 4) (8 , 7) (8 , 2) (6 , 4) no association	(8 , 3) (4 , 7) (1 , 0) (1 , 8) (8 , 0) (4 , 4) (1 , 4) (8 , 8) no association

Scatter Plot Graph

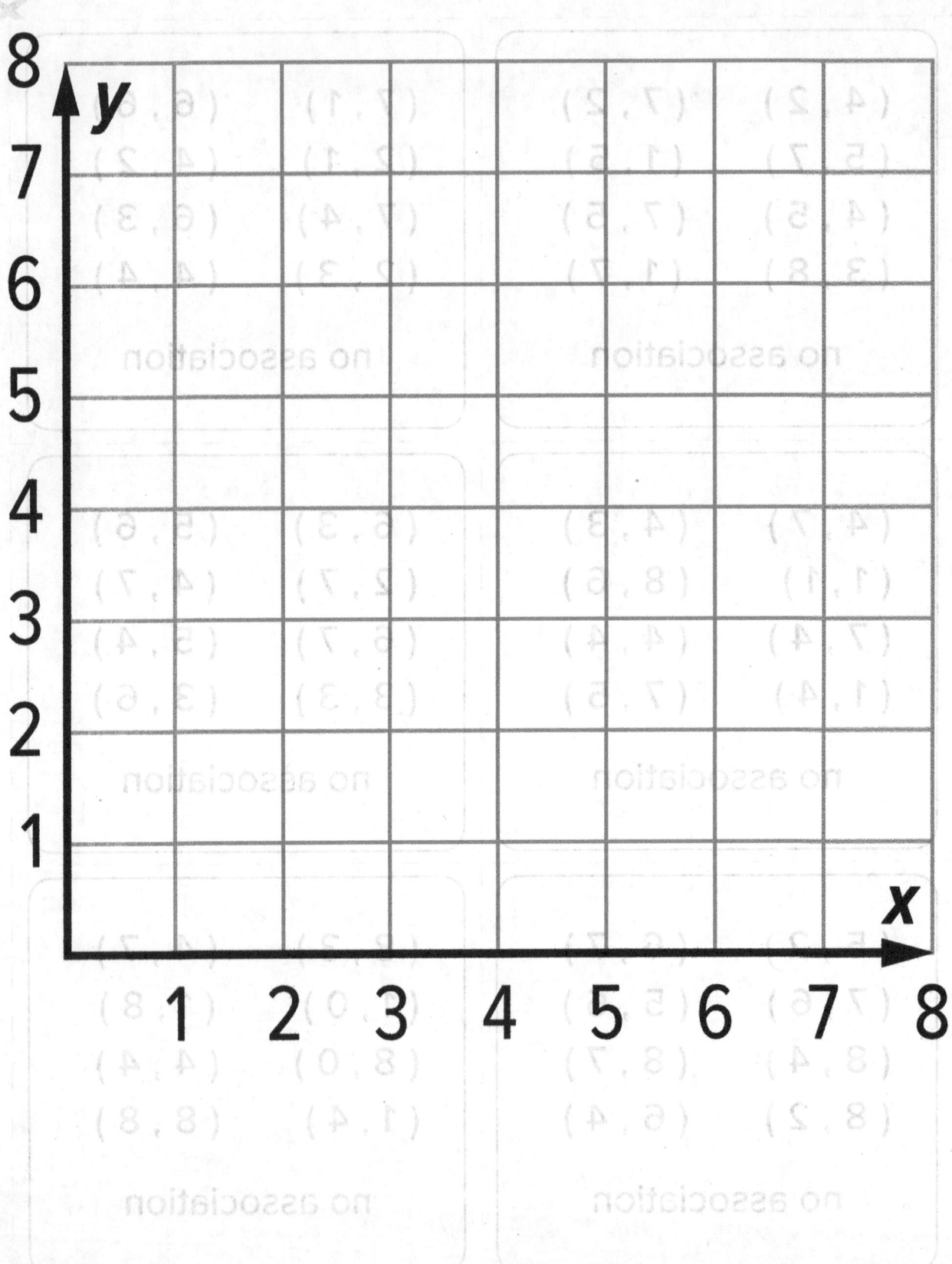

positive association	negative association	no association
positive association	negative association	no association
positive association	negative association	no association
positive association	negative association	no association

Vote Cards

Vote Cards

positive association	negative association	no association
positive association	negative association	no association
positive association	negative association	no association
positive association	negative association	no association